DOOR

Poems by

PETER VIERECK

HHB

Higganum Hill Books : Higganum, Connecticut

First Edition
First Printing, September 1, 2005

Higganum Hill Books
P. O. Box 666, Higganum, CT. 06441-0666
Ph: (860) 345-4103
Email: rcdebold@mindspring.com

Library of Congress Control Number: 2005005121
ISBN 10: 0-9741158-5-1
ISBN 13: 978-0-974115-85-6

Edited by Erin Clifford Carey,
     with editorial consultation by Helen Reeve, Connecticut College and
                              Arthur S. Wensinger, Wesleyan University.

Cover: *Death's Door* by William Blake (1757-1827)

Library of Congress Cataloging-in-Publication Data

Viereck, Peter Robert Edwin, 1916-
  Door : poems / by Peter Viereck.-- 1st ed.
      p. cm.
  Includes bibliographical references.
  ISBN 0-9741158-5-1 (alk. paper)
  I. Title.
  PS3543.I325D66 2005
  811'.54--dc22
                              2005005121

Independent Publishers Group distributes Higganum Hill Books.
Ph: (800) 888-4741   www.ipgbook.com or www.calliope.org/hhb/
Printed in the United States of America

DATE DUE

Demco, Inc. 38-293

AN 2 3 2006

Acknowledgements:

Some of these poems appeared earlier in the magazines Agni, American Poetry Review, Atlantic Monthly, Boulevard, Harpers, Humanitas, Massachusetts Review, New Yorker, New York Times Op-Ed page, Parnassus, Evansville Review, The Formalist, New Letters.

The poem "For Brodsky," in Part Two of this book, won the New England Poetry Club prize for "the best poem of 1998."

"Small Fry," in Part One, was awarded the Anne Sexton prize in 1999 by the magazine Agni for their "best poem of the year."

Dedication

THANKS to the following who have helped me so generously and so thoughtfully on the manuscript: my son John-Alexis Viereck, my daughter Valerie Gibbs, my granddaughter and literary executor Stephanie Gibbs, my granddaughter Sophie Kim, Sonya Roberts, Betty Falkenberg Viereck, and Deborah Kearney.

CONTENTS

TEM PVS

VIRTVS·SOLA·ACIEM
RETVNDIT·ISTAM

PREFACE: Autobiog
(born N.Y.C., August. 5, 1916)

I.

At four saw seagull feathers
Trampled on Hudson piers.
Soldiering, saw others.
Naples. Algiers.

Born on Riverside Drive.
A weed no asphalt could kill.
First verses at five.
At it still.

They asked me at six what I'd do for a living
If I had a future to purchase.
They heard my reply with misgiving:
"I'll be a clown who builds churches."

I've moved far from that outburst,
But it is never far.
Crasser sweets have stoked my thirst,
But sweet they never were.

Church without clown?
Unleashes ayatollah.
A grin without icon?
Unleashes Coca Cola.

A reverence that smiles: I need this mantle
To hover without wish, and mild, and gentle.
But hubbub lashes out at me and rips
The feather of sereneness from my lips.

So I take "stands" and brawl and vaunt.
It is – it isn't – what I really want.
I, ex-fetus: homesick to be in
Womb's sane asylum on earth's looney bin.

Everyman surfs some kind of perilous sea.
Sea's inner kind feels sharkier to me.
Pratfalls? Not just by clowns. By Everyman.
Isn't that *la condition humaine?*

Ban clowns, ban arts? They – soberly – lure to the brink.
Bartenders don't drink.
The poignant laughs that matter
Are – ouch – no laughing matter.

Uneasy rests the clown that wears a head;
When all's law and order, he sees Pan-ic ahead;
All's organized, sealed safe in foolproof sheet;
Help, what breaks through and runs on naked feet?

Your build-a-man kit. A good sport, well washed, noble browed.
Glue together these pieties. Gorgeous bunk.
He president, guru. Adored by crowd.
Till clowns laugh him apart as plastic junk.

On my watch in the Thirties, in Russia, in Germany,
Secret loners had to metamorph,
Grabbing their own faces and peeling them off.
. . . That old gray nightmare, she ain't what she used to be.

New kind of nightmare: first we're saved
From chore by gadget, then enslaved
By tech. "The road to hell is paved
With good inventions." In nuclear sunshine bathed.

I warred for the American
"No" to the Mustache and Genghis Khan.
Ism-wars are a bust,
But these two were a must.

This brief free-mind "must":
More, more than futile pose.
Our tiny conscious dust
Outshining big blind cosmos.

My "conserve"? For freedom-centered ranks,
Not for southwest-of-center plutocranks.
State-goodies for biggies? Shouldn't surprise us.
The socialism of the free-enterprisers.

What's "free"? Not state's free lunches.
Define "human"? Robot that's conscious.
Only man (beasts have safe reflex-chain)
Has knack of being able to go insane.

Dictators? Wounds that strut on steel.
Jackboots hide Achilles' heel.
Slaying Goliath, you become his clone?
Dave, break that cycle; smite with your harp, not stone.

Adam spat seeds of apple-knowledge out.
Look, what fills sky with mushroom cloud?

II.
"Life," can I love you? – you slow-action poison I ate.
Love earth? – one of the uninhabitable planets.
And a wrong-headed pa? And a wronging wronged mate?
I love you each, you memory nets.

How entice enticer?
With pasts my past is littered.
Love hasn't left me wiser,
Just more embittered.

Yet isn't it something to have been
Called "my beloved" now and then?
Catching – quick, quick – a hand to press
Just before my heart bypass.

My warmth is now charred air.
Am fading; dream me back soon.
Am unreal; dream at me harder.
Meanwhile I'll bay at the moon –

– Discreetly. I've learnt to bay with proper
Herr Professor civility.
No lies. I've rarely bayed a whopper.
I tell truth slant like Emily.

My verse truthed forth a better planet's spore
And grew it next door.
Offbeat wildness, in strict form stashed.
Selling like cold cakes. I write for the past.

Or is it the future writes me forth? I'll be
Back when your grandchild jump-starts my poetry.
In times of cash and yawns, with art in tatters,
The resonance of lyric form still matters.

Not mechanized form, that net without the tennis.
Free verse? "The artlessness that conceals artlessness."
My prose books? Mostly remaindered.
I might as well be brain dead.

If write what rage requires,
Would riots make me stop?
No, stopped by bored non-buyers.
I might as well close shop.

But while demagogue woos and cult is quick booze,
Wordcraft's the durable muse.
When those idiots crown me, who foretells
If it's with laurels or bells?

Sure, I've delusions of grandeur.
So do you, *hypocrite lecteur.*

    III.
Maybe on other worlds "living" re-happens.
Here we take turns at it. No choice; no weapons.
Birth battle, death rattle, refrain that deafens
Creed's defense.

We turn-takers eke healing song
From the pathos of this refrain.
But whatever it is that's feeling song
Can also feel pain.

Only old knows life. Too late to live it.
Knows when to change. But too stiff-kneed to pivot.
An exile from my own autobiog,
I leer at it through senior-citizen fog.

Like trusted hound, gone suddenly rabid
And hunting hunter instead of rabbit,
A mobile abyss from my trusted hearth
Is hounding my heart.

*   *   *

Whether 9-to-5 deals or soused at three A.M.,
Babbitt senior or junior both boast freedom:
"We're nonconformist individuals
Like everybody else."

Reversing such slick colors of my eon,
I am a rogue chameleon.
But when I've adjusted, boostered, blustered,
I got, like the General at Little Big Horn, Custered.

I've sought, since the Battle of Wounded Me,
Safety in shell: a turtle.
This traps me in walls I can't hurtle.
The jail of self: shell's entry fee.

When death's Custered pie hits face,
Let go with grace.

IV.
Go? My green hangs on unweakened
Till tailgated by fall.
Then shared mulch, fecund,
Connects us all.

My selves trans-selved: last leaf
Joins mulch. Relief.   (August 5, 2003)

5

LOOK! – TWO-LINERS FOR TWO-TIMERS.
(When there are two speakers, one is in quotes.) (Some lines are
duplicated in the longer poems.)

PAIRS
Lives seek a second chance, alone in pairs.
Look, aren't we all two-timers unawares?

PAN-IC IN METROPOLIS
(After Stefan George)
All's organized, all clothed in plastic sheet.
. . . Look, what breaks loose and runs on naked feet?

DICTATORS
Look how they strut, these supermen of will,
These cripples. Jackboots hide Achilles' heel.

PROGRESS
What has the tech age left the soul for food?
Look for the road kill crushed across the road.

SPROUT
The seed of that apple: Adam spat it out.
Look up, what's this mushroom cloud?

DIGITAL CLOCKS
Look Ma, no hands; continuity disappears,
Chopped time becomes the Muzak of the spheres.

PARIS
Henri Quatre thought Paris worth *une messe.*
Helen of Troy thought Paris worth a mess.

HISTORY OF REVOLUTIONS
You slew Goliath and became . . . his clone.
Dave, break that cycle – smite with your harp, not stone.

AGNIS OR DEUS?
We thought a Lamb was in the shed.
We face a bull with lowered head.

STALLED AFFAIR
We thought love's feathered symbol cooed our love.
Caw; an albino crow is not a dove.

BONDING
You long for actions to restore our bond?
Kick off these sandals, stroll across this pond.

SOCIAL WORKER'S IMPROVEMENTS
Bacchus? Send to Al Anon for aid.
Venus? Fix her. Call a spayed a spayed.

"RELEVANT" POETS
Plastic tears? – red ink on with-it page.
Art's blood writes for the ages, not the age.

LAW OF METRICS, LAW OF LIFE
(tribute to Wilbur)
"Nix on rhyme. Free verse frees stronger passion."
The strength of the genie comes from his bottle's compression.

CRAFT
"Magic that believes itself" – is bunk.
Art, being bartender, is never drunk.

NOVELTY
"What kind of novel is my existence?"
The only kind that ends in mid-sentence.

INTIMATIONS OF MORTALITY
"I'd flow forever if I were a torrent."
You aren't.

ACTUALLY
"So what do we actually get from the arts?"
Arts. Star. Tsar. Rats.

STING OF THE SPELLING BEE
"Arts live! Spell those two words once more."
Vile rats. Tar's veil. Evil star.

SALVATION BY ISM
Pox vobiscum. Blatherly love.
World botherhood. A Trojan dove.

REALPOLITIK
"Bang bang. Steel's not just for agriculture."
When I hear the word "revolver," I reach for my culture.

LA CONDITION HUMAINE
From outer demons, I took refuge in
Armor. And found them stashed inside my skin.

REAL MAGIC
That you are this to me and I am that to you
Makes 9-to-5 a daily Xanadu.

BUT GODS
The leaves we trod will tread us, their mulch a two-way portal.
"But gods?" – All gods *were* immortal.

TWO STRANGERS LEAPING TO DEATH FROM BURNING TRADE TOWER
(9/11)
We million watchers paused – was it a trance? –
When we saw them hold hands.

SPIRIT AND DUST
(reversing Angelus Silesius)
We don't know who we are, and what we are we're not.
An unthing and a thing, A circle not a dot.

AMBUSHED BY JOY
Short moments, cherished for still shorter years.
Why have I suddenly burst into tears?

UNTRENDY
"Your fem cult, your rhyme cult, they're both antiquated."
What lasts is always outdated.

THE MEANING OF MEANING
Fem means both meanings of "to bear."
Rhymes resound, connect, contrast, compare.

OUTLIVING MY FRIENDS
Each new loss.
"Is" to "was."

PART I

Door: Out and Return

"Returnent Franc en France dulce terre." – "Song of Roland"

"Keep handclasps (while we last)
Warm. We cool fast." – from "Crab" in Part I

SPONDEE

1.

Like halves of a spondee[1], the two kinds of footfall
Stress. Both meanings of stress. First
Her warmth. Later (far behind her?)
The tick tock of reap.
Clocks tick, bombs tick, but she –

2.

– Hangs around; sunsets let go slower;
Eyes meet eyes and bind.
The laurel and the vineyard always knew her,
And even our traffic jam can't block her tiptoe:
Old as the Foam she's from; new as, say, Laundromats
(She'll mate stuck sock).
Confined by walls, can tap with breeze;
Called "blind," sees with lap.
Demands twice everything yet doesn't need to be earned.
Define her? Wax and
Terrible iron. I think she *is* rhythm.
Half-glimpse of April and pubic hair.
Forgive us our *non*-trespasses.
I think she is trapdoors; only traps can set us free.
So light her tread that gravity's outwitted.
When stairs are endless, she is endlesser;
Scared of her shieldlessness, they can't stop her.
Leaves fall back up from her mulch. Snows
Don't.

3.

Footsteps nearer. The knock at my door.
She, the waited for. Oh

. . .

No. Treading heavy ahead of her,
The snow fellow, her tick tock shadow.

(June 2003)

---

[1] Spondee: a verse foot of two syllables where both are stressed.

EROS AND THANATOS

(This jolly jingle is chanted by two clowns made up as Harpo and Groucho, doing a soft-shoe shuffle together.)

We're Eros and Than. We gets our man,
Our caper subverting whatever you plan.
We're Harpo and Groucho of slapstick fame,
Love and Death our stage name.
Come close. At first our aim
Seems just to entertain.
       Yes, nearer still – it's just a game.
       It blows your mind, the stunts we offer
       And the celebrities we ham:
       T., for example, puffing sulphur,
       E. walking on water.
       Our pair is what you're feeling
       When dark is light – a healing;
       When light is dark – a scam.
Lured close by our deceiving,
It's now too late for leaving.
We're in you before you can scram.
"Dignity"? – forget it.
"Free will"? – don't give it credit.
"Life"? – a skit we edit.
Helen eloping with a jerk;
Kid hit-and-runned by van;
Yet light unclouding now and then:
It figures who's at work.
       E. flows, T. ebbs; the referee
       Is tide. It's a duet of three.
       We're flotsam and jetsam; tide gives and takes back.
       We always gets 'em; we're ruin and wrack.
       The one is the fire, the other the pan.
       "PLAY," says Eros. "PAY," says Than.

(1999)

OLD VOYAGER

Who says the housebound has no adventures left?
Every rise from my chair is an adventure.
Every trek to the next room is a dangerous odyssey.
Each staircase is Everest.
Now forward still more forward,
Half-speed ahead.

(2001)

SOMETHING RELENTLESS PUSHING ME

(Speakers: myself and then – in italics – earthworm)

1.
Let me go. Am very business.
By the way, just what's the time?
"Dust time. Busy under."

I can't hold on: a leaf, a life,
Falling. Anguish ending?
"Anguish starting."

Have I time to grow a lawn?
"Above too late. Below too soon."
How soon my soon? – *"A quilt."*

My quilt, will it be brown or green?
My sleep, will it be cold or warm?
"Warm cold green brown. Push."

It's me that's pushed. Relentlessly.
"Me too. Earth code." – Whose push? From where?
"It's March that's pushy. From under."

Chain reaction. I'm pushed, I push.
Why and what must I garden soon?
"Just as relentlessly."

Earthworm, my ultimate earthmom: can't I fly?
*"Shut up and push . . . I reject you. You're
My child no more."*

2.
A bird on my shoulder. Dove or crow?
No, too big. A singing swan?
"Vultures make nice pets. Until."

The arrow can't return to the bow.
But love – can squandered love bounce back?
"The dog returns to his vomit, the leaf to its mulch."

Whatever's returning, I'll cleave to love's clinging.
"Cleave has two meanings.
Cleaver just one."

My blades of grass, are they sown by caressing?
"Blade: two meanings.
Under: one."

Knives, are they made for friendly tickle?
"You'll gash green blades
Up through brown quilt."

O what of lawns all fresh and upward,
That early Eden eeriness?
"That busybody chore. Guess whose."

I crave sweet rest. Will dead dust doze,
Free of chore's rack at last?
"The pity I thought I lacked prevents my answer,

My darling tired child."

(1998)

16

A MEDDLING SLEEP

To feel a centipede on your neck and not feel it.
To see lightning but as black, not lit.
Your grave-dunked sleep,
Though nicknamed "endless," isn't deep.
Your labyrinthine mole-creep
Is far more active, gulped by turf,
Than on the life-waves you'd scant time to surf.
You do and do.
As gracious hostess, being impartial to
Guests, you feed
Alike the flower and the weed,
Just as faint rays from far Aldébaran
Neutrally stroke each rival earth-clan.
Give earth a break; stop tickling her peristalsis
To force forth green's summer solstice.
You're both the down-wormed and the upward daisied,
Shared snack of acorn, bug, and hay seed.
Yanking the leaves down and the Aprils up.
Gray dust yet golden buttercup.
You're Pied Piper for starved rat,
Catnip of sweet meat.
What should be grow-joy is rot-eater eaten by rot.
Frisky cadaver, you resound
All over the place with discord-sound,
The busybody of the underground.
Birds, when above you, tweet off-beat.

*   *   *

At last the last dust melts. Now peace!

Returned; beautiful. Yet unease.

(Nov. 9, 2004)

17

Ex Nihilo Nihil

1. *The No-Word*

Now that all galaxies are mapped,
We've all the facts and nothing true.
The No-word "nothing" is the clue.
That all must fall was nothing new.
And knowing this, we nothing knew.
What wine can vats of nothing brew?
Our lives are contracts where we pay
And pay – although there's nothing due.
And though the contracts are a con,
There's no Contractor things can sue.
Fists flail at No but never through.
The day when man caught the fever-flu
Called "consciousness," storm's nothing blew
All nests apart, no nestling flew.
Since then, we're scattered; no things glue.
On Venus-calyx, no more dew.
You've had your fun, now face her pimp,
This hit man hiding in her loo.
This reaper with the nothing-hue,
Scythes you at nil's annulling cue.
Yet all's not vain whenever you
        Guess vanitas is you.

2. *West Rays*

All growth ends as if nothing grew, –
The acorns many, nuttings few,
The torn threads many, knottings few.
When sunset-rays come knitting you,
Red hirelings of nevermore,
They're spidering round you, netting you;
What can a spiraling gnat-thing do?
Don't think you'll sneak from nothing's view;
In paranoia's nutty zoo,
Two zero eyes are noting you.
Nought's left to add your nothing to.

Some hide inside love's Xanadu
Of nothing-me and nothing-you.
Twice nothing is a nothing too.
What plus can hugs of nothing woo?
Day, at the edge where two realms mix,
        Says "always," Night says "nix."

3. *Caveat Lector*

These rhymes, hypnotic spells for you,
Drone on, – narcotic, two by two.
All's sleepy – hey, you're nodding too.
When reading refrain's nothing through,
Take care lest it be reading you.

*   *   *

Lucky are you who, tricksters all,
Goose earth till she unnothings you.
Though preachers boo from nothing's pew,
Taboos cannot out-nothing you.
But in the night all nothings rue,
These sound-repeats come numbing you.
These nothing-rhymes you're reading now
Are whirlpool-traps your merry crew
Right now (too late: you've read too far)
        Is sinking down into.

(1999)

CALYX: VAGINOLATRY

(male author's voice is unindented; a woman's voice in quotes and italics)

> *"In westciv must I bounce between*
> *Shrines and the smut on walls of latrine?"*

Your gender? Too smirched – and too prettied – to fathom.

> *"Unsmirch. Ungentrify. Then we'll illume*
> *Things unattempted yet in prose or rhyme."*

Ending each line of our she-poem
With the suckling letter, the mom letter, the 'm'.
And then with the war letter 'r' as counter theme.

> *"Labia. Lap. A calyx wisdom.*
> *The wound that heals wounds. Welcome*
> *Back to your lost first home."*

Calyx as soul zone? (The erogenous zone is the cranium.)

> *"Nothing stays in. Male enterers? Brief flotsam,*
> *Staying no longer than, say, some tampon jetsam.*
> *So go in peace; Tampax vobiscum."*

The final Enterer stays. With scythe, not condom,
He reaps all death-denying hokum.

> *"Here's what can't die (despite the womb-tomb syndrome):*
> *This orifice's cornucopian maelstrom*
> *Of generations, all creation's mainstream.*
> *This one-eyed stare: a Cyclops in a cave dome.*
> *This four-lipped yawn of immemorial boredom.*
> *This timeless whisper to each new callow bridegroom:*
> *I am my granny's granny; time makes numb,*
> *But the location! Such a slum:*
> *Two garbage-dumping neighbors, I between them."*

Anatomy plays cruel pranks on queendom.

> *"To punish her. She foils the scam*
> *Of anatomy's loveless breeder-scheme.*
> *So nature throws her not some balm*
> *But a custard pie as a terrorist bomb."*

It's dribbling down her face; I honor her aplomb.
O anyhow queen! Her 'anyhow' paradigm
Is self-surpass beyond our simian kingdom.
She alone made it natural to overcome
Nature. Hence my homage – no, femmage – to femme.

* * *

"Where exit and entrance join in tandem,
Apes have it easy. But femme's nine-month waiting room
Gets wrenched aching-wide. (For baby's big cerebrum.)"
That crescent as half-moon: two wobbly full moons roam
Around it. They bounce in high-heeled tum-ta-tum;
Whole hordes of whistlers, a sniggering bedlam,
Watch from behind. She's not demeaned by them.
Louts can't make phoenix dim.

* * *

"One fragile little fur-lined seam
Will ever be in final sum
Unrest's rest and ransom."
Are Sphinx and sphincter then the same
In the riddle of the spasm?
In Molly Bloom's 'yes,' in Saint Teresa's psalm?
Can meat be soul; by awe made awesome?
Are paired physiques less physical than they seem?
Then flesh transfigures flesh in tangled twosome,
A cat's-cradle, woven on a four-legged loom,
Transfiguring but never transcending loam.
    "It isn't real, you know. Charade. A game.
    I fibbed; I drugged you with odeur de femme.
    Plus Muse-mush. So don't make my gender your nostrum."
Your sudden reversals are your abnormal norm.
You, a her, belittling her: how come?
    "What's wise about my calyx wisdom
    Is that it debunks 'calyx wisdom.'
    My who-I-am trashes your what-I-seem."
You talk plain English when males spout hot air.
Goad us to take you as you are.
    "Calyx, though more than sperm-spit's cuspidor,
    Is less than wisdom's door,
    Lone flowers wilt. Calyx needs stamen stem.
    So don't cry over spilt milt.
    Male milt does more than Milton can
    To justify God's ways to man.

21

'Calyx wisdom'? I said it. But it's mere
Saws like 'wipe from front to rear' and 'wear
Absorbent underthings in summer'."
'Under.' Evocative word. Caressive? Sinister?
'Under' and 'over,' somehow they're each other.
From under winter, April weather.
We all know who shares Pluto's lair;
Wherever under and lofty share
One center, she is there.
"And isn't. I spoofed it all. A slit-skirt lure."
No, no, her lore is greater, though unaware,
Than wildest spoofs could dare.
There are wisdoms none can bear to bear.
"My lap bears the spoor
Of the dreadful iron of God. A brand-mark bloodier
On Eve than on Abel's brother.
That hour, tell me, did God's nostrils flare?
Say, did God's macho scepter rear?
Weren't they heady enough, His rites of yore,
Lamb's neck outstretched, eyes trusting, white throat bare?
Did sky crave kinkier fare?
Cervix in Latin means neck. Did God the Ripper
Cause Eve-neck's unhealed scar,
Now every woman's sacrificial altar?
The countless breach births. Each Caesarian scimitar.
All labor pains. Eve's future torture.
I feel ten thousand coat hangers abort her.
She shrugs – it's the pluck of the fragile – and combs her hair."

> *   *   *

Her Scar forgot to close. That flash of slit pink –
Across grave's knowing wink, across the night's black stare –
Makes even death blink.
"The word 'pink' lacks gravitas.
So do final -ie and -ess.
Girlie panties lack dignity."
They're not reduced by reductiveness,
I'm in awe of how regal their skirt-rim.

22

"Godd-ess and girl-lie are sisters under the hem.
And both must lift the hem to pee.
Your fem cult, your rhyme cult, they're both antiquated."
What lasts is always outdated.
Rhymes resound, connect, contrast, compare,
Fem bears both meanings of 'to bear.'
    "Replacing mariolatry, you've decreed
    A daft coinage, vaginolatry."
The only idolatry whose idols need to need.
    "Our need for make-up! It's really an upper
    Underwear. We feel so open, so
    Above below."
As soft and invulnerable as slashed air.
No jeans. Skirts have a life-affirming flare.
Life, come to me glass in hand; ass in skirt;
Sassy-voiced; moist.
    "She-ness envy is what you suffer from.
    Venus envy plus Persephone (Pussy-phoney).
    A composite she. She as fulcrum."
Around this fulcrum loves and seasons swarm;
Grant me, like rafts to ships in storm,
Her seesaw equilibrium.

    *   *   *

    "Females don't flatter femininity so.
    (We wish our botched zipper were Velcro,)
    You're no mere 'feminist'– you're feminist-ad-absurdum.
    Males are the best Lesbians. The best dildo:
    A flattering pen. . . .Of course, deep down you're macho,
    A very patriarchal gigolo,
    And don't mean a word you say. But you're welcome
    As troubadour for my double-X chromosome."
Your realism is your opium.
What's surreal is you, the self you don't know.
    "So what's my inner stranger, who or how?"
As bitter as surf, as pulsed as a far drum,
Calyx is still the source we're orphaned from,
Relentless rhythm, tide itself, the hint
Of grail all pilgrims hunt.

"Don't speak mystic. Speak blunt.
Speak English. Do you mean wet cunt?"
'Speak mystic' and four-letter-English are not at war.
Both scorn cant, both voice core.
    "Look, whether calyx, stamen, cranium
    All things human are slaves of shame and sham.
    Moon bullies tide in queendom's monthly thralldom,
    And nine months rule the two-way slot machine.
    . . . But stop, – what's this spun coin within my skin?"
This orb of all that's random
Spins on with fate's momentum,
The doom we're flipped by when we flip a dime
Where crossroads loom.
Male pollen gambles on her inner spin:
Roulette of gene.
'Va banque'; win egg or die; few swimmers win.
    "Big lotteries – between just two small knees –
    Can win a Nero or a Nazarene."
Losers lose and winners lose. Skies tease
Earth with absent-minded butcheries.
    "I've tried to face them with aplomb,
    But their unfairness leaves me numb,
    A vet of endure, of loss an alum."
We're all wary strangers, gender or clan,
All same and unsame, linked and lone,
All scorched – while feuding – by aging's slow arson.
Then burn – with touching fingertips – as one:
Toward the shared loam we sprouted from.
Like pairs holding hands as they jumped from a Trade Tower room.
    "What's 'God' but a bouquet of wonder, rose, and random
    Bomb?
    Let rose mean whatever you want it to."
It means the petaled healing I'm compassed to,
The only sentimental lie that's true,
From flower to trope to troubadour to you.
    "Like sad and porn, red roses all are blue."
They change to Furies when gypped of rose's due.
    "Hell hath no woman like a Fury scorned.
    Then even petals are thorned."

Lap, for your neonates what hopes are near?
　　"All hope abandon ye who . . . exit here."
And so each nine-month lingering ends,
In past imperfect and in future tense.
Lap's archway, why are you arching, why our parch?
Launch us beyond the flesh, bow of that arch, –
　　"– to beyonds only flesh can reach."
What's left us? Roots and continuities?
　　"Tempered by gypsy laughter behind the trees."

(2002)

LOVE , (THE BEYOND OF PAIR)

(same two voices as in "Calyx," his unindented, hers in quotes and italics)

Monstrous: the weight of earth's green thumb.
Unfecund tenderness, brow to brow,
Is it *contra naturam*? Yes, yes, and maybe no.
A yearningless tenderness struck me dumb
When once we were sitting apart, just watching a garden bloom.
I feel the same (how mesh the two?),
The same and not the same,
When I overflow in your undertow
That tows me above-through-below. I owe
A warmth I can't repay to a depth I cannot plumb.
　　"I owe you my warmth: for a peace I can't reward,
　　The beyond-the-flesh that only the flesh can record,
　　The seedless yearningless beauty abhorred
　　By earth's fecundity yet part
　　Of her all-inclusive hoard;
　　Provided it sweats, not even brow is barred.
　　Pistil and stamen as trio: the third the beyond of the paired."
These green beyonds, they're jinxed from the start
By their entry fee, an armorless heart.
If you want to go beyonding, drop your guard.
　　"And join the scarred? For the Hallmark card
　　Called 'love,' pair's loony ward?
　　No and maybe yes. I'm sceptic, I'm scared.
　　And yet and anyhow
　　I consecrate to the great 'What if' my brow
　　And my petals, my own sweaty greensward,
　　For the garden of spirit we, sitting apart
　　And anyhow joined, once shared."

(1999)

26

I. Letting Me Down

The leaves race by me at the angle
The wind decrees, and those that dangle
Won't long hold on.
I've just plain got to write of autumn,
Now that – for me – July's post-mortem
Becomes my own.
The old guy whose attention I can't wangle,
The patriarch of Up, he's let me down:
Not by being bad but by not being.
If he'd be, if he'd be, if he weren't fleeing,
Could he reverse my downing?
Leaves have luck; they need no gods for bouncing
From mulch to March.
Me too? – No hope. I can't match mulch.
. . . Is everything really permitted if
There's no upstairs? My downward skiff,
Smashed on life's cliff, needs clasp of other: –
There is no God, and Mary is his mother. [2]

II. Shimmer

And where the thousand angels on the pin?
One angel still exists, the hint of green
In the red of setting suns.
And awe through nights and wonder through noons
Rack me with hints of more than matter,
An upward fall, abyss as ladder.
Unseeables seen.
"Triggered by self-surpass is dust transfigured?"
Is. Into something sometimes somehow more.
Still mortal. Still this-worldly as before.
Not dustless transcendence. We're all mud's descendants.
Yet in our murk the 'more' is not quite gone,
A tear of wistfulness on cheek of stone.

---

[2] Line from Santayana's remarks to me in Rome, 1944.

Dust-glow: it's the great 'anyhow'
Against the low of less, against the west of 'must';
Godlessly godly; 'despite' against night.
"Does it make sense?" It makes music.
The shimmer cascades from rock to rock;
The fierce rays shiver with joy of shock;
I've savored (not all flamingoes are plastic) a panic
So beautiful it left me serene, it left me scared; –

      There was that lake. The moon's reflection yearned upward
      From its sunk mirror. I must haul.
      But winds, amok, churned waves of squall,
      A horizontal waterfall
      I stared at. And it stared.
      . . . Then, like remissions in a cancer ward,
      The winds grew gentler, the ripples shorter.
      A shiver of joy; peace, peace; a liquid altar.
      It didn't make sense. Yet whatever it made, I had.
      I was the net, and every strand was glad.
      I pulled the moon out of the water.
      It wasn't heavy at all.

                   (2000)

LULL

(to Betty in our winter)

We wading off the strand.
Then – wham – a fluke-wave's whim
Slammed us down.
Gagging on mouthfuls of dune,
Half drowned, half on land's brim,
Bleeding from tidal rake:
We sand castles, downed on sand.
But not for keeps. We're grateful to have gained
The lull in tide wave's wake

     Too grateful. There's a price for comfy lull.
     Our peace was never "peaceful."
     What loss did gain incur?
     An inner brine, blood's rancor at too serene an anchor,
     Slammed all our treasured linkage
     Down into winter's rage.
     Too late for sun when two are less than one.

How stoke a cooling moon?
Old age's fortune wheel
Spins wounds that never heal,
Healings that always wound.
Skin wrinkled, winter pressing; throat turtled, trees undressing;
Flowers with icy sandals; our sand castle a sandglass;
Confetti of time-grains endless;
The wheel relentless: Betty, Betty,
Where to?

     We're driftwood, once in tow
     Of one wave's vertigo,
     But – after sea let go – an ashen moon's our prison.
     Remission of wave's passion
     Has lulled our linkage too.

But up from some obscure
Unquenchable core, the cure
For lull's too bland décor
Keeps on, keeps on recurring –
As long as we keep caring
Enough to plunge below unnavigable flow,
Hugged down down down by undertow –

    – And up. More alive for being half-drowned and reborn.
    Don't think they're safe, the half-alive, who hide
    From elementals, huddling in port and norm;
    Some waves can reach inside.
    Some terrans are Antaean not to terra
    But tide, – we born umbilical to terror.
    Risk that plunge. Tide is both chaos and form.

Retrieval? Though moons of aging shine unwarm,
Comes link, comes love, outfluking fluke-wave's storm.
Come, post-green wistfulness,
Gray as the hair and wrinkles we'll cherish now.
Come flabbergast what's left us – eke from less
More – eke core from loss.
Because of all that's gone?
No.
Because of what keeps on.

                (1999)

CRAB [3]

(Mostly my voice, addressing a young friend with cervix cancer. Her voice in italics and quotes.)

Each in our way, according to our scar,
      Falls far.
Does, when its tired clasp lets go, a leaf
      Fall with relief?
Such different scars; so similarly banned
      From Disneyland
Edens of health. I wish we'd some incensed
      God to play Job against.
"We two: complicity of the stricken ones?"
      In hospital once
Our terminal eyes, our brief fast-fading hands
      Met with the glance
Of drowners drowning rescuers. That's how the dead
      Wed.
No more than a clasp, no closer intimacy;
Not mates, not kin, we're yoked into a "we"
By some encoded sunset lingo. Be
      My Linear B.
"When doomed pairs clasp, an anyhow hangs on a cliff
      Of if.
Old youth and age: joint package for Under. Expressed
      West."
But green, but blue: so sweet a globe above ground.
      Stick around.
"But red but rot: a leaf lets go with relief.
According to our scar, each in our way
      Can't stay.
They've opened me nuder than nude all privacy gone.
      I loathe my own drained lean
Red meat. Crab play it. It's his violin,
The bow his claw, the strings my nerves of pain,
      Metastasis the tune."

---

[3] The Latin word for "crab" is "cancer."

31

When most demeaned, it's then you're most a queen,
Redeeming from cliché the dignity of "human."
"When Crab like a gondolier beneath Venetian moon
        First serenades a woman,
He strums from her cervix nerves a wistful strain
        As languid as morphine.
The fondler lies. Now hear his true refrain: –
'All flesh rots and stinks in the end' . . . O then
        End me soon."
Rot always wins. But which all does it win?
        All mulch grows down
And up. Now hear, each time you're death-wish-prone,
        The red-leaf-mulch refrain: –
'Your grace-in-pain, when most in mire, in strain,
        Is LOAM, is clean.'

        *   *   *

No chumming with chummy patients. Their hurrahs
        Are our alas.
"Peer group"? "Supportive" pap? No, better can't
        Than cant. . . .
"Can't? Our clasp can't shorten by an hour
        Crab's power.
Only my scary radiation lab
        Stalls Crab."
Between reality's cracks, you're slipped by radium volts
Into a science-fiction film for dolts.
About some Frankenstein madman. Whoosh, he jolts
Your startled bones with high-tech lighting bolts
        That frisk like colts.
"If that is comic relief, it won't relieve.
        Spread-eagled on a slab,
Exiled without reprieve, I still am Eve.
This time no fig leaf where the scalpels jab.
        If but each stab
Were life! Blood always was birth's cruel price-tab.
But Crab, Crab is crueler still: the birth
        That isn't birth.

The child that is no child. The invader-breath
        Of a stowaway death."
A war zone on the operation map,
        Your Armageddon lap –
Holy, messy, stubborn – is earth's last stand.
        O resist to the end.

    *   *   *

        "Hearing Crab's guffaw,
I panic from clinic to clinic. From Rome to Arkansas."
When traps close, desperate wolves chew off a paw.
        Here it's your soul you gnaw.
"The what you see is not the who you saw.
Now Crab, not Eros nests where I feel claw.
A jealous god: 'All others keep out' is his law,
        The rapist who won't withdraw.
For my lost spores – my beauty's barren flaw –
I'm autumned by earth (sky's erogenous zone) as outlaw.
I'm midnight, she's aurora. She's grass, I'm straw.
All year's for me as frosty – am I a chilblained Kora? –
As half a year for Pluto's half-signora.
I've lost, like far dry mountain-cooped Andorra,
The tides of earth. I've lost my link as daughter.
No binding mortar. A knife in the gut cost me terra."
You're still her child, her blood in your aorta.
Her tide keeps flowing: from wet nurse, madonna, squaw.
        "Ebb is my era."
By she-right for the she-wrongs Eve foresaw,
By right of eons of lap-toll paid to moon-law,
By right of all who mutinied in the maw
Of their biology and lost to Moira,
Reclaim – like red regreened by primavera –
        Earth's green-red seesaw.
"The entropy-knife of rot it shreds like coleslaw:
        Her red-green jigsaw.
Leaves can't go on. According to our scar,
Each in our way, we serve the leaf-stink law."
        Yet touch is mulch law.

33

Touch – reclaim – your loamy mother; rip her bra
        Of ice; with awe
Touch – suck erect – her thousand tits of flora,
A thousand nectars of nurture. She's coo plus caw,
Eros plus Thanatos, white dove, black daw.
        Inhale her aura
Of sweaty gender. With bitch tenacity, draw
On the strength of the she-wolf in the wolf-trap's jaw.
Dream impossible warmth. Feel, feel (where frost raged raw)
        Thaw.

        *   *   *

"I feel my young hair grayer every visit.
My toe, as if inveigled by a wizard,
Is dipped in Styx. But not my hand – or is it?"
My clasp, being free of womb's Crab, is it free of radium's glow?
        No.
Radiata outreaches dentata. It's. reaching me. now.
The whole room tilts. Solidity has been scissored,
Shedding limbs like a lizard. We both are fissured and flow.
"I am a human Chernobyl. Am I Adam's femme radi-fatale
        Or Pluto's moll?
My skin, translucent porcelain, casts no shadow."
The refrain is: each in our way, according to –.
        But I can't go
On. Am sleepy. Is sun the only light?
        "Crab's dark beeps bright."
I'm yawning, I'm yawning. Keep handclasps (while we last)
        Warm. We cool fast.

                (2000)

DELICATE AND FRESH

Are tears, blood, urine, semen, musk of she –
Above all, tears – brine beached from fecund sea?
This woman's dammed-up tears: linked bitterly
With her unfecund seed?
Or with bruised girlhood, from the start ill-starred?
Which wounds decode her chart?
A self-styled monster and kind: which the key?
Humane without humanity,
She, warming every child in need,
Stays cold. Cold fire as the art
Of parting with an all-too-human shard
That won't depart.
She's passion-charred all over, except one part:
Her armadillo heart.
Brutal – no, bitter – her candor (by her own armor scarred): –
　　"I've let down my pants more casually than my guard.
　　But tenderness is nuder; is both stripped soul, stripped garb;
　　Is core, is hearth.
　　How melt me the vulnerable wistfulness my hard
　　Guard barred?
　　Bared trust; the one adventure I haven't dared.
　　Sea mother, wronged too often: too long I've been your orphan.
　　I'm autumn-in-spring. Make me your spring-in-autumn.
　　What's hymened is my soul. Rip it open for a new start."

　　*　　*　　*

At once her tremor. Writhed change,
Sloughed shell, sloughed chains.
From deep abyss, a tall surprise.
Blood the sand and heart the sandglass,
Trickling to the foam-born goddess,
Who completes the incompleteness
Both of lust and ice.
Tremor: she must dare dive into that foam,
Saying "amo" as before it became cliché, –
She fresh and delicate now; fall's Lazarus May.

From farthest skies a frozen lodestar cries,
"I am all warm inside. It's not so far across."
Her tremor: doubt's or awe's?
With elementals now her laws, her loam,
She thaws – from that day on – the long way home,
As tears yearn back toward sea.

(1997 - 2000)

For a Rumpled Loamy Soul

(The "she" is President of the "Child's Play Institute" for sick youngsters)

I.

"Can a woman forget her baby?" Isaiah said.
Can a woman forget the baby she never had?
"Child's Play" is now her child. She, having none,
Is living the verb of "mother," not the noun.
Her barrenness is Baroness of Styx.
She's pregnant. With the cancer in her cervix.
"Child's Play": her safe-house for the troubled young.
She would have somehow hid each infant victim
If she had been around at Herod's dictum.
On the Titanic she would have saved the drowned.
Except herself. In each reincarnation
She battled demons (her own) who always won.
Nine lives ago she lived in Borgia town,
A chic Grand Lady whose provocative gown
Concealed a hairshirt that excruciated.
Divorced adulteress, excommunicated,
She is and isn't Catholic, more faithful to her faith
Than moralists whose holy-water bath
Cleaned them skin-deep only and created
Nothing, rescued none.
Her many selves enshrine more gods than One.
A maenad nun, she serves both Gaia and God,
As once when body and soul were still one mix, –
Mud eked from bloom and bloom from mud.
Half sphincter and half Sphinx, a mud-stoked phoenix:
Her loamy earth-soused kinks
Are not the bricks but the mortar for sky's bricks.
Though Crab now dominates the dominatrix,
She has a shield: the very human chinks
Her pride conceals within her armor links.
What's humanness? A sweaty alchemy.
It changes – into eerie melody –
Our rotting meat that aspires, aspires, and stinks.

*   *   *

37

She's Leonarda da, the multi-talent wonder, –
Her own Pygmalion, carving herself as myth.
But marbles, not marble mark her classic grandeur;
Too many ironies in the fire;
Hers the stretched length of "genius," not its width.
Wow, what strong will! – too willful to compress
Her every-which-way drivenness,
So overreaching that its "more" is less.
Her "quick" is too overextended to quicken. Her eyes,
The two in her skull, the wounded one at her thighs,
Are too smart to be wise, too poise-pursuing for peace.
Her child-care does stupendous "good"; no pose.
Too good at work, *Too* good at love, these hide
Panic. Three fates she can't yet face:
The tomb, her final office space;
The tumor, the only lover who stays inside;
The unborn child who, because *not* inside,
Strangles her with its birth cord and can't exist.
To serve as exorcist,
To whirl the craved distraction of her rounds,
A lot of desks must overload,
A lot of bedsprings bounce.
Pilgrim on knife-runged road
Of treadmill's nowhere-race,
Slow down. Home base
Is where the Grail was always stowed.
She's never where she is. Then what's her sole repose?
Her books, her well-wrought prose
As troubadour for the hurt and the disowned.
With words and deeds a founder; her self she never found;
It's rented out on public lease.
And yet her "and yet" cuts loose her core from sleaze.
Her "anyhow" is anyhow her solace
Against what sullies. Unless – .

*   *   *

The way Saint Denis lugged his severed head
After that martyrdom when it was shed,
She lugs her martyred lap from place to place.

Not lovers now but surgeons trace
Her lap with scalpels, lasers, X-rays.
What once was private, now is map outspread
More public than her face.
Her "dignity"? It's that she just keeps on
Crafting her books, bossing her office, healing the young,
While bearing the unbearable all day long,
That secret hairshirt under sensuous lace,
A Catholic pagan American saintless Grace.

*   *   *

The wingèd thanks of children swarm round like butterflies,
Wreathing her breasts with rainbowing allies.
Sweet: the thanks of those she saves.
Unsweet: each hatched from pelvis not her own.
New wingbeats suddenly. From caves, from caves.
Who gibbers, who squeaks? Their leather wings blot sun.
White bats, the progeny she couldn't spawn,
Nip her dry breasts and fade as ghosts at dawn.

II.
She plays a twice-played tragedy,
One barren and one fecund enemy.
The second stuffs like Christmas stockings what
The first forgot.
Crab brings as Santa Claws with gift-wrapped taunt
What least we want.
This telepath – what we all dread he knows.
Some dance, some laugh; it doesn't last;
We end aghast.
Now back to where I rambled from. The birth-throes
That aren't birth. Like all starved embryos,
Crab grows.
Red the sand and black the sandglass,
Bleeding toward time's final sea.
What I keep calling her "bitch-tenacity,"
Can it press wine from lees? Can she lose loss?

* * *

West gate and formcraft interlace.
"Create" defies "non-procreate."
Her gender's wounded stare locks eyes
With the abyss;
Rivals since DNA first squirmed from clay,
They strive as duelers in the deeps,
And which prevails awaits her dive.
The brink. She stalls. She skinny-dips
One toe in destiny. She sheds like clothing
Her devil of a self-love that's self-loathing
And (worse) her angel of public pieties.
Scene shift. Trance landscape. Snake-crammed bogs.
When such as she outbrave such odds
To chase through knee-deep silt
Our future's ignis fatuus,
It's then she zigzags straighter pasts for us;
She's building ancient roads before they're built.
Meanwhile our petty cares.
Meanwhile the petty stars.
Mere galaxies across mere infinite blank flow.
She, petty like us, is yet our undertow
To an Above below.
One wisdom her many ignorances know:
When Techno grooms us hairless, flawless, neat,
When it shaves moonlight from the moon,
Watch out: what bursts the coop and bolts on furry feet?
Trance, and her dives from crag. Does she often bungle, drown?
Her deaths the running gag of a slightly immortal clown?
Not so; like us at abyss's brink,
She's the usual human mess; yet link
To elementals with whom we're out of sync.
So fallible a link, half girl, half crone.
So . . . "rumpled" is the word. Call her a lone
Dryad on the lam, without a tree core.
Trapt, stript, and spitting. Her oak's been bulldozed for
A mall by Progress raging
As amok as usual. The trance is raiding
My sleep. Her paleness. Gales. Wild horses racing.

She self-ignites. A flesh-torch flaming,
She's her new red-haired twin, escaping
Toward water, all three eyebrows blazing,
The elementals re-embracing
Their frailest, their most daring plaything,
Who's never more than human, never less.
She's sloughing off all more-than-human dress,
Layer on layer, god on god unfolding.
Here's Baal, here's Dagon; look, there's Zeus, there's Odin;
The rags of the spooks of the creeds of ages past;
The beautiful love-bearing son is the very last.
And now her dare of omen and foreboding;
Her ultimate dive. Into low loam, outsouling
High cloudiness. A mud bath molding
Low-rooted tall epiphanies.
She dives into and through – beyond – abyss.
. . . Or doesn't. Is her scribbler friend
Hallucinating some fake vatic end?
Either way, for her he's always Here.
Because she leaves earth earthier
And never lets down some snot-nosed brat who needs her,
Her friend won't let her down . . . Her friend? Who's he?
Drop sham – who writes these lines? – it's me,
Calling her – from now on – "you," not "she."

III.

We've learned what bonds to tighten, what to sever.
I know you too well to be what's called a lover,
Not well enough to cease to explore your maze,
Your one-eyed lap, your two-eyed face,
So twined they seemed a single blaze,
A Medusa turning me not to stone but moonlight.
Not one, not two; no, what defied
The enemy inside
Was the triple stare. I called you Argus-eyed.
When first you unveiled the lower gaze
(Sad-eyed wit, ancientness of rite),
How quick you boasted, "Look, I'm guilt-free, guilt-free."
Too quick. I decoded – behind bravado's cover,
Behind the worldly smirk you wear –

41

What you don't want me to discover:
A pitapat heart, a tight-clutched rosary,
The high-voice high-mind hymened wisp you were,
Starched in your first Communion dress:
A scaredy-cat princess trying to look gracious,
With girl-scout cookies for the deserving poor.
There's something this phantom of this child of yore
Urgently wants me to bequeath:
     "Friend Peter, the future I run from is a tree
     Where opposite no-nos split the pith.
     Pretty-please, twine them in a single wreath."
But look, the apparition starts to writhe.
A baby boa in wrath? The "boo" of a child-wraith,
Or a cuddly vampire? Giggles hiding teeth?
What's tickling my jugular? Only a breeze's breath?
Either way, being already so near my death,
I fear no phantom. My protective sheath
Is that there's nothing left to kill me deader with.
. . . All's norm again, Macbeth
At Birnam, Lear on the heath,
The usual blood-mess, all flesh being "afterbirth."
Your Crab, my age, they dunk us both
Home into earth.
But somehow we're intenser underneath
The final surgeon's scythe,
And your abyss now breathes me when I breathe.

     IV.
Your cheeks. Two sea shells, worn hollow by mumbles of sea.
Cancer drugs. Nausea. Puking your way across three
Continents; tailgating every quack remedy;
Then back to . . . metastasis.
Such horror from such wee drops of telltale blood.
The blood's not on that white Communion dress.
It's on more rumpled a dress that communes with a darker god
Who knows your wound; he *knows*; it's not by lot
He picked that spot; he's your setting sun;
By your pubic hair he's dragging you down –
Through pasts – to below the horizon.
Hag of three thousand years – spread-eagled in Babylon –

In Salem hanged, in Rome a hairshirt nun –
A dozen times burnt at the stake for your compassion,
Heretical miracle-cures of the hurt young.
That rosary – clutch tighter – you, too, a child on the run.
For your fifth birthday you put a pinafore on
With frou-frou collar and asked for a hot cross bun.
Now ask for a month from my bank of time.
I'd add what little is left in my credit card
To your bank of life if I could.
I can't. To you I accord
Rhyme, a dead man's valentine
To your Decembered June.
Your stains. Two kinds. The black one
On soul. The red on gown.
Red the sand and black the sandglass,
Draining toward time's last alas.

               V.
Some children think a wound goes away with a kiss.
Futile? Of course. There is no winner.
Futile. But near your friend you wait serener,
I driving out your drivenness.
Meanwhile that stare, your gate that can't beget:
Now Jack the Reaper's scapegoat.
He's at your gut. He's at my western gate.
At, at. At his – at Jack Frost's – tether of ice,
Are we (honed twice: by worms, by weather)
Already dumped in the same ditch together?
Already cadavers? – dreaming we're forever.
Two skeletons straddling each others bones? – with fervor
Fiercer than flesh's much-sung fever:
Skeletons having more apertures to savor
Than mere raw meat can enter.
When dead ember, rubbed against dead ember,
Re-ignites December,
Are we each other's necrophiles? – the "one night
Stand" that stays through all nights: meaning never.
. . . Tourists of our own future lightlessness,
Wait-listed still for our subsoil address,
Arms full of broken toys, we loll at the dark river.

43

But then, like lightning through that dark, I glimpse
What you so rashly squandered on the winds,
Your ornery inner light.
Then waste so lavish grows a savage ripeness.
Then, having rightly scourged your wrongfulness,
I marvel that such wrongs can be so right.
Because your stains can't stain your stainless aura,
It takes no lover's praise, no child's hurrah,
Just me, your skeptic friend, to know
Nobility of soul. And so
I'm only Here to bless, dear Deborah.
. . . To give your staring wound this futile kiss.

(1998)

DESCENDANT

"I've landed. Make way for man" - spoken by my ancestor, the lungfish, in a poem in *Tide & Continuities*, Univ. of Arkansas Press, 1995.

1.

After my mutant seed dislodged
From sea these brand-new lungs I lugged,
I still felt racked. When at last I walked
Two-legged, the sky that stalked me lagged
Not much. The day my thumb extended
(To grip a throat, to grip an ax-end)
Entropy's taunt, that Torquemada accent,
Never slackened.
Am racked eternally, – not fatally;
Skilled torturers don't kill.
Through each dead shell, my rogue genes still,
Like evergreens in fall, hang on
(I wish they fell – it's PEACE I wish) and spawn
An Auschwitz and a Parthenon.

2.

After my Cretaceous trammels,
Exit dinos, enter mammals.
Enter my Cro-Magnon annals.
I'm the rogue chimp – me me me –
Who invented agriculture,
Fire, wheel, and caveman sculpture,
My eyes now eyeing inwardly.
That's why for fifty million years a vulture
Pecks my Promethean brow apart.
Vulture? Call him nature, call him nurture, –
My seed jinxed from tile start.

3.

Down in an abyss that blackens,
Here is Egypt, there is Athens,
Crete overgrown with brackens, Ur with ordure, –
All my pasts one junk-strewn yard.
Ecce homunculus. My tightrope slackens.

Inward eye was my debaucher;
Must all beast-innocence depart?
Sister, witness of my torture,
Beacon of my art,
It's from you deliverance beckons
As my waning moon wanes paler.
Once each thousand years of peckings,
As revolving earth-clock reckons,
You distract my feathered jailer,
Feeding him a hunk of your own heart
To give me peace . . . for fifty seconds.

(1998)

TIME ENOUGH

1.

An old man with flowers
Is loss without sorrow.
The big orb that batters my small orbs with light
Is telling me something: Scattered dust regroups
Toward arson. Love's arson? Combustible once more
Is my rekindled all-too-senior dust.
Wine out of lees?

2.

Who phones us each just once and it's collect?
Losers lose and winners lose.

3.

Where do all the atoms go?
While my teeth convert lamb into me,
Earthmom-dentata is munching me back into earth.
And my last moment is only a moment but
A long-time moment: car-wreck time.
Time enough for me to hum (please listen)
Highs out of lows.

4.

Humming a flower that never existed,
Smelling new rhythms to make them exist,
Sometimes I'm not afraid to die.
An old man with rhythms –
A dust-heap with flowers –
Is loss without less.

ANTAEUS AGONISTES[4]

I. ANTAEUS AT 19

(written as Harvard student, 1936, unpublished before)

1.
Silence, nineteen silences,
Till boredom's yawn outgaped abyss.
Years of hush except for clocks.
Not deeds but books.
Nineteen years my asbestos soul
Lolled cool.
But now the lightning, crouching in the cloud,
Pounced loud.
Though now combustible and armorless,
Yet rotten-ripe now to aggress,
My future entered then. From when?

2.
Who's there?
    "Your bootlegger."
Which speakeasy?
    "Sobriety."
Not genius? – "That's a dime a dozen;
    Just judgment, that's the rarity.
    Say can't to cant. Lucidity
    Is grape. Fake depth is raisin."
Must I sleep? I'd rather wake.
    "Some deeps are unfake."
Cant soothes top.
    "Below won't stop."
Your curses, why so crude, so lewd?
    "To desecrate righteous platitude."
That ax, is it for chopping trees?
    "Not . . . for . . . tea parties."
That knife, to open mail for me?
    "Not . . . only."

---

[4] Greek myth: Antaeus could only gain strength by touching earth, his mother.

Why those brass knuckles on your fists?
   "To bully bullies (rightists, leftists)."
You shout me down.
But drawing rooms
Soon disown
A voice that booms.
Your self-promoting boasts shock wincing hosts.
   "Proper Bostonians? Harvard Grotonians?
   Don't think your soft-sell swill fools Beacon Hill."
Burglar alarms – I hear them clang.
   "Your lynch-mob gang of anti-gang."
It takes whole mobs to teach you outlaws laws.
   "Or crown us. Either way with flabby paws.
   . . . Too sane a student, tamely earning A,
   Confront the price-in-gut you pay."
Ingot we trust, our bank notes say.
Your price is hang-ups, lowing darkly.
   "The more the merrier. They're what sparks me."
Stop compensating for being so gauche a lout.
   "Guess whose delusions of grandeur I'm acting out."
Ouch. I creak in every joint.
   "Call me teen's turning point."

         3.
As I looked closer at him looming there,
Horror tantalyzed my hair.
He was my double, hair to shoe,
Except his eyes (they panther-green, mine blue).
"Ham actor of other people's lives," I cried,
Raging inside;
"Arsonist of souls, don't hex a student's nest.
My books are lightning rods against your blast."
   "I have no time," he smiled, "for chatter
   With those who – well, no longer matter.
   The wranglers tug me. Can't you hear them howling?"
   Said he scowling.
   "The strong besiege me," said he – unalarmed;
   "I am a weakling, very strongly armed.
   I, from this instant on," he said,
   "Become alive. And you? Were always dead." He said,

"Your gut is sending me to you
To take your place. Get out. I've work to do."

II. ANTAEUS AT 80

Touch was once my healing.
Mulch bounced back fallen spore.
Now, when I reach for Gaia,
All I can clutch is air.
Give back, O give me back,
What I never had: earth's core.
Now when it's time for me to fall,
She'll touch me, not I her.

III. ANTAEUS ORPHANED

1. HOVERING
No longer here. I'm never.
I now don't am. I hover.
Why plunge so deep in lap and loam?
Because I'm wind's fluff, nowhere home.
I welcome love's most poignant scar.
It makes me feel I'm meat, not air.
To prove my solidity isn't fake,
I welcome even a toothache.
I can't cast shade because no core.
Can males be dryads, tree their lair?
Stash me in oak. I'd grow
Roots, core, shadow.

2. EARTH'S BORROWERS
My tryst with Romany: black eyes and white
Teeth of the palest, blackest-haired of daughters.
Henna you prinked by Andalusian waters,
Dawdling – with scorn's grace – south of wrong and right.
   O you
Laughed sun back hundredfold like caressed dew.

And did you, past my sonant fruit-tree strolling,
Hear hundred wines of air compel you back?
Then what a mist of longing our enfolding! –
Fused myth of dew and wine, each other's lack.
    O may
Coastlines of contour rise from mistiest spray.

No cosmic wrangles crowning either Prince,
Not all the stakes of soul for which They clash,
Are worth the angel of a lucky glance
That casual earthlings in their glittering flesh
    O throw
At daily things, – rain's tilt, or sheen of snow.

In earth who wallows like its borrowers?
What bodies can so sensuously press
As bodiless phantoms? Touch-starved fallowness
Can yearn the very sun loose from its course.
    O would
That ghosts, through lust, earned shape. If but we could.

I know you now! No Romany your home.
Then know me too; no Arcady my lair.
Formless you flash; I hope you, and you are.
Weightless I hover; need me, and I loom.
We secret twins, we mutually hoaxing pair,
    O we
Never were. Back home to hell come flee.

(2000)

SISTER

I.

A mistress's hand I don't quite want,
And mom-style hand I scorn.
The magic that works is a sister's hand.
I'm hinged to that shelter's warmth.

A different warmth from "lover"
Or rough-and-tumble "brother."
More spoused to me than spouse, yet walled
Farther from me than far.

I know all this because – complicity:
We shrink (not kill) our parents
Into jade one-inch godlings,
Handy as paperweights.

She was a holy and sassy waif.
Sisters are older than brothers, especially when they're not.
She gawked into green distance with
Raccoon-dark eyes, the sister I never had.

Deepdown, boys crave bravado delinquency.
Sisters crave rules, made soft by caring.
Our sharing was: let's climb that tree
And how haha all grownups were.

. . . More grown, she gave me a loamward shove:
"Lean on the wind. If you flop. it proves
Mud's gravity loves the mud you are.
Inhale this rose. Yup, deeper. If it thorns you,

It's to prove you bleed blood not machine oil."
A shove with brake. *"Nix on boy's outlaw-strut.*
Burst free but stash your lib in laws.
Run wild, no uptight wimp, but with strict wildness."

II.

She is – no, was – my trampoline
Toward what? She was – no, is – no, is –
The hand I clasp (though it isn't there)
In surgeon's waiting room.

Alexander through the Ishtar Gate
Toward final fever in Babylon
Was not more driven by drivenness
Than handclasp's hand toward hand.

A clasp through the terrors and toys called "child,"
She was my fever and its cure,
Cool fingers on my eyes.
I remember her well, the she who never is.

She is, she *is*. She, you:
More really mine the more unreal you are.
I'm hurtling backwards, younger through the years.
From the slingshot of now, I'm skimming the pond of the past.

Splash. Blub blub. From drowner's flashback give me
Just one innocent child-day shared.
Prayer answered by a scared and strutting boy
(A deepdown self I don't dare face): –

"Hey Sis, let's trash the school down, wow,
And scram into our tree house and
Pee down on the whole darn lying world."

(2002)

TO MY UNDERTAKER

"In Licht und Luft zerrinnen mir Lieb und Leid!" – Hoelderlin.

Prepaid cremation. File my receipted check.
Come, longed-for furnace; dissolve into air and ash
My backpack of flesh. Let soul, a weightless flash,
Leave earth below, a sloughed-off rash.
The flesh-pack drags soul down; cremate means create.
. . . But what, but what if behind the backpack,
No back?
Then honor backpack. If it's all that's there,
Then circle it back down home – don't waste it on air–
This boomerang of loam. Dust as dust's heir.
What wings it is its very winglessness,
An unbeyonding grounding; transfiguring, not transcending;
Outsouling, not unsouling.
You funny little man, whose smooth palaver
Peddles pricey coops for my cadaver,
Don't think you're my true undertaker. Earth is.
But will she ACCEPT me if, opting for fire,
I cheat her of fodder?
Then nix on cremate. With hearse gung-ho at my gate,
I'm changing my deathbed mind: quick, cool that furnace grate.
. . . Oops, too late.

(2000)

THIRD TURNING POINT

I.

Blue and gold of October.
River's swift silver.
For millions of years creatures couldn't see.
No eyes. Couldn't see shadings, shinings.
Couldn't see mates.
Sight, the first turning point, happened in sea.
So casual. Oh, it should have been with
Sea-quake
Of foam-queen being born, bringing
Armfuls of colors.

II.

Second turn-point: from out-sight to insight.
"Who am I?" There should have been
Thunder of Promethean chain-break.
Third turning: a beyonding.
From "know thyself" to self-surpass.
Icarian hubris? Of course, but this time melting
Not wings but sun's will.
Even then, plenty of petty:
Card tricks, malls, prettified lawns.
But still the trans of transcend, a spread-ing fan
Op-en-ing ho-ri-zons.
Jungles moving. Where to? Gardens,
Watch out.

PRIMAVERA

"Giovanezza, giovanezza, Primavera di bellezza."
                                    – marching song of Fascist thugs

Too many poets write about spring.
Today, presto, she appears in person.
Tainted all over with the leprosy called green.
Bulgingly pregnant with the monster called life.
A hag muddied by too long below,
Forcing acorns up.
Quick, stop her from jarring awake
Loam's peaceful drowse.
She's squeezing forth, she's strangling forth
These weeds, these thorns.
O give me autumn back, the mellow fade.

WELCOME HOME:

1.
"MY LOST CHILD – "
"Is back. They chased her with stake and chains.
I'll hide her safe." – Returners change.

2.
THIRST
"My long-missed baby. 'Kith me,' she lisps."
Long dead. Fanged lips.

3.
REPRESSED
"Nothing unnerves me. Name something I dassn't face."
Two sets of bloody dentata. One in each place.

CLICHÉS RE-AIMED. MORE TWO LINERS

JOHN HANCOCK
"She's quit collecting my autographs, I wilt."
Don't cry over spilt milt.

DRUNK ON YOUR VERBOSITY
"Oh wow, my poem's inspired by sheer inspiration,"
Don't operate machinery while taking this medication.

TRAFFIC COP
"Who's driving with a scythe behind my car?"
Objects in mirror are closer than they appear.

OUNCE OF PREVENTION
"She's hiding her swelling, but I've got a hunch."
A stitch in time saves nine months.

ZEUS LANDING ON EARTH IN "LOHENGRIN" SWAN-BOAT

"Natives," he shouts from his swan-boat two-seater,
"Take me to your Leda."

MUTUAL SLANDER

Lib pot calls kettle black. The gilded
Crackpot calls the kettle Red.

"FORGIVE US OUR TRESPASSES"

Lovers crave invasive caresses.
Eros, forgive us our non-trespasses.

PROCRUSTES THE IMPROVER

Praise zigzag and mess. A straight line is the longest
Distance between two points. (And the bloodiest.)

"DON'T LOOK NOW, BUT SOME ONE'S FOLLOWING YOU"

It's my assassin. No, only my own
Shadow. Or both: each other's clone.

HELL PAVED WITH GOOD INTENTIONS

We need to be freed from what freed us: Technology.
Invention is the mother of necessity.

"ROSES ARE RED, VIOLETS ARE BLUE"

Like sad and porn, red roses all are blue.
They change to Furies when gypped of rose's due.

PLUCKED ROSE

Hell hath no woman like a Fury scorned,
Then even petals are thorned.

PAST IMPERFECT; FUTURE TENSE

Womb, for your neonates what joys are near?
"All hope abandon ye who exit here."

UNMERRY-GO-ROUND
All ends. Burst suns keep deleting us.
No end. Big bangs keep repeating us.

*   *   *

THIRD WAY
"Progress or ivory tower?" – Scorn both abysses:
The uplift scam or the Snigger of the Narcissus.

DONNE-HEMINGWAY: "FOR WHOM THE BELL"
Loners are wiser than brotherhood mobs. Whole
Lives are half island. Not all bells toll.

A CURSE ON BOTH YOUR BLOUSES
Two witch hunters, right and left. Each makes his pitch.
Which is witch?

SPOILSPORT
"What are you, jabbing your friends and your own party line?"
Chameleon in reverse. Plus porcupine.

UNDERTAKERS' SECRET
Do you know that these ashes you tenderly strewed
Were mostly not papa but burnt coffinwood?

DENDROCIDE
The wind stings your eyes with the ashes you strewed,
Spiced with sliced dryad from oak's coffinwood.

SCHOOLBOY'S HOLIDAY (ANCIENT ROME)
Dad took me to my first crucifixion. A loud
Salesman hawked treats to the good-natured crowd.

"MAN," OF COURSE, MEANS WOMEN AND MEN
Man invented not merely God but "humanity."
Gods are a dime a dozen; man's the rarity.

GOD SPEAKING
That biped I botched, it got out of control.
Next time no soul.

TO HIS ANGELS
Stop loafing on that pin, goddammit.
Go fetch my lab a fresh new planet.

"ANYTHING GOES"
All civilization, gone in a trice,
Is a pirouette on melting ice.

YET STANDARDS
"All's relative to class, race, fad."
Some things are just plain good or bad.

TERTIUS GAUDENS
"You're mine," mind preached. "No, mine," pain screeched.
They wrangled. Time sneaked up, mugged each.

NOT QUITE ALWAYS
Sky is always. We're all almost. We're
Not quite hyphens to there from here.

THE ANYHOW OF ALMOST
River of reverie, silvery sliver:
Brief comet (called "love") you outlast mere forever.

SMALL FRY

(*sic semper*)

Brer Edwin – forgive – I upstaged you, your famous role as
    Macbeth.[5]
Both times – we're both performers – the theater held its breath.
They say the new Duncan was saintly, and maybe it's no myth,
But he assassinated my south, my south, my south.
Let Harriet Beecher blubber, let Horace Greeley whine.
I did it and I'm happy. I butchered a Yankee swine.
Their hounds are on my traces. My ankle hurts me so.
I was always derided as little. I doubt they're laughing now.

*   *   *

Oswald, Sirhan, McVeigh: my future's unhatched seed.
Ah and my superclone Leaders; what future states they'll lead!
Comrades, *Volk,* blest marchers; ah what a heady broth!
How many little-town Littletons are time-bombs ahead?
I'm land-mine Lazarus, exploding when dug forth.
Where lies cast out the outcast, there only my bullets are truth.
Anoint me the winningest loser, sweet Violence, savior of earth.
Come hate me, you mobs, all you want to, but never dare *judge* my
    deed;
Too high the voice I follow. Resenter or martyr? – I'm both.
In vain, in vain they'll hang me. How hang the never-dead?
I'll live in headlines, in schoolbooks. There sons of your sons will
    read
(It's what I really yearn for) the name of John Wilkes Booth.

(1999)

---

[5] *Macbeth* was favorite play of both Lincoln and the Booth brothers. A few
days before his assassination, Lincoln read aloud to friends the lines "Duncan is
in his grave; / After life's fitful fever he sleeps well."

PART II: Gate Talk

These new and related poems are the culmination of the many Persephone
dialogues in the author's two preceding books.

I. ZAGREUS IN BEDLAM, 1889

(The Greek wine-god Dionysus was called Zagreus: "hacked." The grapevine's branches were hacked in fall, regrew in spring.)

I.

Mostly hexameters: to twine caesura'd needs.
Some lines shorter: to pace my speeds
For two rival gods and a mortal who bleeds.
The god of vine: his seasons giving what seasons take.
The god of love: his Passion hauling his wood uphill.
The mortal, a loner, chose vine; thus he, Zarathustra, spake
His half-truth. Versus half-truth from that hill.
When truths are capital-lettered, duck when the boomerang zaps.
Don't get Truthed at; Eternities in caps
Lapse.
What lasts? One instant of beauty. Beauty, not pretty frill.
My teacher-pair: messiahs? No, not carved stone but seeds.
Here not to drug but wake
Our lives to learn to live a livelier life.
Protean credos, not Procrustean creeds.
The snowflake of joy frisks over their "all too human" ache.
Joy for its own brief sake.
Till Inquisition – in black or Brownshirt – feeds
In each cult's name a stake.

II.

An empire, pregnant with God, squeezed bawling states from her
　　　　womb:
Madrid, Paris, Rome.
State plus stake imposing the love from the wood on the hill.
Long trails of carrion, hobbling, veterans of the stake:
Another resurrection, will they stern-browed return
To tear down all cult-prisons with hands that horribly burn?
Wronged ghosts are judgement's earthquake:
Who these on the chimney-smoke, up from the Nordic urn?
North's Santa-kitsch reversing the two-way chimney stack.
Teacher-two had warned: don't hate ("a vile mistake")
The race of the one on the hill.

III.

The poet of love: ever healer, despite our hates and wars.
His sermon's mount outlasting all mount there ever was.
Yet leaving weapons arming both sides of every cause.
Lights have dark cores. Because there's no because?
Both searchers pay their search's excruciating costs.
The Twilighter of Idols lurches on mania's course,
Alive within mind's corpse.
And hill's love? Ends on cross. Dove that not coos but caws.
Its clause of "meek inherit" is a caress that claws.
No unearned Santa Claus.
No sky-gods till tuned earthwards
By beauty, strummer of nerve-cords
Forwards to harp-chords. Isn't
Unwizened beauty deities' deity?
Oh for nightingales in Galilee.

IV.

The poet of Dionysus, balancing "know" and "lo!"
The wounded Herr Professor, replaying "wound and bow."
He muddled the superman plague of twentieth century.
But twenty-first needs him to nudge us from techno conformity.
His dynamite frees with a quip.
For the complacent, he's insomnia de luxe.
His one-liners stun books.
Yet his fireworks lack plain practicality.
And he doesn't understand women. (Neither
Do women.) A scared boy: "For woman, whip."
It's he got whipped, of course. By syphilis, sister, and Lou.
(Why don't I name him? Labels tether.)
No mind more daring than his, outgrowing ever new.
Outgrowing: God, man, country, Wagner, self.
The chaos that tunes chaos. The sick who exudes health.
Three pastor-generations of conscience-bite so ruthless
He probes it beyond good and evil, honing old morals toothless.
Immoralist with hairshirt. Grape-crowned, yet saint disguised.
Finita commedia, '89; dark clown's last "no";
Ecce the Anti-Christ.
Gently the thorn-crowned asks him, "Why do you wrong me so?
Give me your hand. I was ever. . . the hacked vine Easters regrow."

(March 2005)

64

NOTES ON MY SECOND TEACHER

Some readers insisted on these notes; let others skip them.

Insane: from 1889; syphilis; died 1900. Lou: his love-hate Lou Salome. Ode to a Nordic gas urn: he warned his country in vain against the future menace of anti-Semitism. "Dynamite": a nineteenth-century invention, made just in time for him to use as a favorite metaphor. Twilighter: he coined "Twilight of the Idols" (Goetzendaemmerung) as pun on Wagner's "Twilight of the Gods" (Goetterdaemmerung). "Ecce" ("behold") and also calling himself more clown than saint: from his book *Ecce Homo*. "Finita la commedia": from the doomed clown Pagliacci. Proteus: the shape-changer. Procrustean: forcing into rigid patterns ("bed of Procrustes").

II. For Brodsky

While trying at age 84 to survive my own heart attacks, I'm writing these re-inventions of dying for Joseph Brodsky (for, not about, not to) who died of a heart attack in 1996. He was fascinated by the shuttle goddess Persephone and urged me to write more about her. Two speakers: myself and a woman of blurred I.D. card, – her voice (Persie's) indented, in quotes, in italics.

1. AT LAND'S END

That strand I pace, its 'peace' is a misnomer.
TaTUM: sea's breakers break
Me. An unlone loner,
I'm crowded – let me go – by tidal sonar.
No intimacy, ankle-deep, can slake
Tide's thirsty cadence. Though faint as moon's corona
(When rays nudge waves), tide pulses every dust-flake.
Two rival scansions argue: heartbeat and sea. Sea wins.

> *"Tide's easy to argue with, hard to convince.*
> *Leviathan-sea gulps heart's iambic Jonah."*

'Catch a baboon,' my cardiologist winks.
'Graft a red heart from a blue-assed donor.'

> *"Broiled in sun's sauna, a landlubber fauna,*
> *You're a boner, a rogue-gene mistake."*

Yet with one goofy hour: as soul's – no, word's – brief owner.

> *"Old moaner, what you'd housebreak*
> *Is language itself, word's bratsy demeanor,*
> *Re-Formed for muse's manor."*

No, for a friend. I bring, as old-style mourner,
My lock of hair for a wordsmith none can wake:
My *inferiae*[6] in the classic manner
For Brodsky's karma.

> *"Accept that coffin's nails. They're dust's last drama,*
> *Its trauma-healing trauma."*

Once one nailed carpenter made all nails quake.

> *"Undertakers still undertake.*
> *Meet Jack the Reaper; the one friend time can't take,*
> *The geezer's sidekick, the ebb no flow can rinse."*

Escaped from ebb, my blood's an inland lake.

---

[6] Lock of hair placed by Orestes on grave of Agamemnon, a reference (as metaphor for poetry) that Brodsky was fond of. Inferiae: ancient offerings for the revered dead.

"Not in enough from surf's long rake.
Tide drinks its drinker when he thinks he drinks.
There is no inland. Never since
A gasping lungfish climbed on fraying fins
Uphill for Darwin's sake.
You're just a landfish with a tumor,
Called 'mind,' your homo-sap diploma. "
My mind's as septic and free as Rubaiyat's Omar.
"But brainwashed while in fetal coma
By Unda Marina. In caul's wet arena
Linking two worlds like a comma,
She dunked you. You the nine-month roomer
In her boarding house. Till birth's subpoena.
The rent you pay is — gender. "
Both saline catnips, womb's and semen's genre,
Arouse love's double-entendre.
"Brine is love's censored agenda.
Not really freed by hips' meander
From skirts to jeans, not really heartbreak's mender,
Love still intones too gentrified a mantra:
'Romeo loves Juliet, Ferdinand loves Miranda.'
No well-groomed manner and no sky-baked manna
But stinky brine is the raw wet core of the matter. "
All groin's in the head, that kinky master.
"Same coin spins tails, spins heads. Brine spins it madder.
Spin, fortune-cookie coin, our luck's commander.
Each of us gets a throw with no remainder.
At first: bright disk of life (men bet men dare).
Soon obol of Charon, exit's mentor
Roll on, fate's penny, computer chip of Moira.
Shine me illusions, coined by Maya,
A fata morgana where pasts are mañana,
Dead myths my living millennia. "
I'm mulched by autumn's hit-men, time's red mafia.
Spin me a dead leaf's fecund mania.
Same orb clanks on, now hub of year-wheel's rotor.
"Now suddenly my breath is shorter.
Whose rock-and-roll across myth's border
Strums my aorta?
It's wine's traveling salesman. I'm his farmer's daughter.

I sprawl, all maenad to his fiery water.
No, that's too underling an aura.
There's just one rhythm all my crops have awe for.
Orb, shudder me the lilt that's Kora.[7]
A zigzag godling: no altar, no ardor
For righteous systems or straight-line order.
My seasons spin in dervish furor;
I was born tomorrow; I'm a sometimes: I'm flora
And frost. And flora's restorer."

And a child fleeing on a roller-coaster
From a dirty-old-man molester.

"Oh that? That was my Pluto semester.
Now spring. I'm spinning faster faster, –
A panting spirit-flesh fiesta.
My turn to molest; I stroke each pasture
Till stalks rise tall in posture.
Till fall, till scythe (unmerry-go-round, spin closer)
Brings closure. Poet, for you I venture
A 'gracious' (condescending) gesture:
I crown you – clown you – with seaweed (starting to fester)
As laureate (no, court jester).
These algae are bays (I mean bells) for your tonsure."

 It's true your cryptic smile can conjure,
But you're no real Gioconda.
You're a bodiless myth seeking bodily contour.

[she dancing round him, strewing seaweed]
"I confess I'm a myth. I plead guilty with candor.
Can't fly like a condor, can't swim like piranha.
I confess I'm a non-exister. . . .
But doom-scarred Existence, a chilblained Cassandra,
Wills-into-being (on Jack Frost's veranda)
My warm April vista.
What makes earth earthly? Gender, MY whirling gender."

---

[7] Kora, a blurred ambiguity, can mean either shuttling Persephone or simply a maiden. Moira: Greek goddess of destiny. Maya: Hindu goddess of illusion. Charon: ferryman of the dead, his fee the Greek coin called "obol." La Gioconda: Leonardo's smiling Mona Lisa. Despite the high mortality rate for immortals, all the above still resonate as our archetypes.

2. LANDLOCKED BRINE

The spring you whirl is an impostor,
The Potemkin-village of seasons, a green plaster.
I don't believe your huckster-goddess patter;
Faith is a lemming pastor.
>   *"Scratch Pollyanna and find tornadoes. My roster*
>   *Balances light and dark like Zoroaster,*
>   *Halves twinned like Pollux and Castor.*
>   *Love twirls my twirling; she's my sister;*
>   *A double-star bevy of astra circling astra.*
>   *Love is a contradictory disaster,*
>   *Brine-drenched lust when flames consume her."*
Through every exit flesh has room for,
From sweat, spit, snot, tears, urine, not from pneuma,
Brine hollers at me like a slanderous rumor.
>   *"Sniff – be sniffed by – the salt aroma."*

*   *   *

Aroma and echo and glow; the trio of flow's terza rima.
All roads lead to Roma, all veins to the wine-dark of Homer.
Sea dawn: flamingoes shooed by daybreak's hammer,
Rising on foam with flabbergasting grandeur.
Tell Venus she's not the only foam-launched wonder,
>   *"Then dusk: black ax of umbra*
>   *Felling dawn's golden lumber."*
Your Pluto lumberjack from under?
>   *"A soothing sea is his subtler Never,*
>   *Tugging me down when breakwaters break away."*
I'm clay. I was always an ebber.

*   *   *

>   *"There is no condom that blocks mortality.*
>   *Contagious. To feel your clay*
>   *Between my legs makes my Forever fray.*
>   *To be a death-infected deity*
>   *Is bitter – is rich – with the intensity*
>   *Compressed from clay by brevity.*
>   *Now my I.D. is true, is fake."*

Tsunamis wake in us both when we're unawake.
Up from a night too deep to tether,
They call and call with siren timbre.
  "Play deaf when undertow talks tender.
  Don't let your blood be your tempter."
It can't forget its lost sea-center.
Jailbreak! My landlocked waters, straining at every trapdoor
Of skin, want *mer* want *mère* the rapture
Of fleeing their leashing tormentor.
  "Stay leashed. To seal me from sea's blue clamor."
I can't. Your role-shifts encumber.
  "Unda is AT me. Is at ME. To sunder
  Me from Olympus. To hug me to slumber.
  Am sinking; some blue is unbearable; my knees shake."
Where's all your queening now? You blubber.
Stand firm, or you can't be a landlubber.
No, run. It's time to forsake.
  . . . What's that? what throat is howling from a comber?[8]
My kenneled brine throbs back. A heart attack?
  "When they hear wolves howl free, dogs bite their owner."

                    *   *   *

Ah Joseph, gates enter us, not we the gate.
I, being older, should be where you are now.
Thin ice your trampoline. Can leaves fall up?
Our meeting in '62: in your burg of the bear.[9]
Later: bringing you to my Yank college.
Our joint course: 'Poets Under Big Brother.'
I secretly called it 'Rhyme and Punishment.'
Today I'm writing not *to* you (no address)
But for you. Some mulch falls up.

---

[8] Comber: a long wave that peaked.
[9] St. Petersburg

70

III. BANTER ON THIN ICE
(Same woman's voice in this dialogue is again indented and italicized)

1. GATE

Why do I hear a shell shout?
> *"Maybe some seeker; seeking you out."*

Out? What's dimming my east with murk?
> *"Some fogs smirk."*

I've oodles of seekers. I put them on hold.
> *"One seeker is always cold."*

I trust familiars. Cushions, colors, bells.
> *"Some things are something else."*

Which else (you're blurred) is my ex-mistress?
> *"No cold seeker. Ask my mattress."*

Then warm me through Act Five. Stay. Wait.
> *"No waiting-room at west gate."*

A bit soon for gate talk here.
> *"Objects in mirror are closer than they appear."*

Beached scion of a lungfish Argonaut,
I want to shine on land, not be forgot.
Will I live to achieve this artist wish?
> *"To shine, fish first must rot."*

When my pace creeps old with dread,
Will you wait with me at the gate?
> *"When your face sleeps cold and dead,*
> *Mortician-rouge will blush you red."*

Strewn seeds bounce back. The two-way of crops.
'Up' and 'hope' almost rhyme. A mulched leaf drops
Up.
> *"First down. As I've said before,*
> *I love you; I love fact more."*

Fact? We're fiction. Each the other's author.
> *"Here's my offer:*
> *I stop goddessing, you stop committing rhyme,*
> *We both less fictive ever after."*

A deal. No more rhyme. But you're drunk on sobriety.
> *"You on magic. Which kind?"*

That of the guild, the noble-browed uplifters,
Won't work. Mine's of the other breed of
Charlatan, the outsider.

> *"Honor the third magic, the wow of the commonplace.*
> *What saves isn't saviors; it's every-day chores,*
> *The miracle of dowdy kindness.*
> *Your craftiness is unkind, is word tricks.*
> *Yet it crafts (being fecund nonsense) beauty."*

That's how I smuggled meaning and form
(In a false-bottom suitcase of feigned with-it)
Right past the deconstructionist cops.

> *"You once were a scandal of wonder, a flash of a what."*

Now not.

> *"Then why try surviving your heart's failed iambics?"*

Only the living can write about dying.
And for terminal cases the narcotic of choice is scribble.

* * *

> *"It's dotingly to shield you that I warn you:*
> *Distrust your dawns. They're insincere.*
> *They're dusk, pretending."*

Pretendings succeed. My dusk is dawn,
Replayed in reverse. A palindrome backwards.

> *"It hurts me to hurt you again into fact. But:*
> *Dear dignified elder statesman, precisely how*
> *Is senile incontinence repaid?"*

Spell 'repaid' backwards.

> *"A spelling bee. Wraith, spell solid."*

S.o.i.l.'d.

> *"Do you savor the English word 'savior'?"*

I prefer the French word 'savoir.'

> *"Do you believe 'Santa' exists?"*

Yes, Virginia, there is a 'Satan.'

> *"While aging into dust, spell 'age'."*

'A Ge.' An earth goddess for dust.
You've many voices, none for long.

> *"D'ya figure, like they say in scifi,*
> *There's UFO Aliens amongst us?"*

Who needs UFOs? I'm more alienated
Than any Martian. And yet as earth-clutching
As my friend, the shade-giving sycamore.
>   *"I'm also a giver. If your straight line could boomerang,*
>   *My givingness would wish you back to May."*
My goingness wishes lines round.
>   *"Only cans get recycled. Professor Life*
>   *Lacks tenure."*
I touched clouds. I made tunes.
>   *"You made! You made! But earth —"*
I talked her, not lived her. So now
Must I lack a giver at west gate?
Some goers don't wait lone. But I?
>   *"No giver, not even that*
>   *Sycamore, has patient enough feet."*
I'll clutch earth all the tighter. Can't let go
Of touching what I can't touch.
An ancient witch keeps phoning me. Where from?
>   *"From the year 2100.*
>   *She'll be your grandchild's grown-up grandchild, saying,*
>   *'You'll be dismantled any day now — but not*
>   *This poem. It will be remembered.'*
>   *. . . Don't take death personal. It's merely that both archways*
>   *Happen to salivate for protein."*
Bon appétit, mom.
>   *"Umbilic snake, slashed off from your birth, returns*
>   *To noose your throat. I wish it weren't so."*
I know you wish. The body language of your crassest
Words is still, as before, kind.
>   *"A life is the short-lived remission of terminal cancer."*
Then more pressed grapes, then more pressed lips. Fill, feel.
>   *"Yes, press. Yes, harder — No, too late.*
>   *Countdown. No Act Six."*
Anyhow press press press.
>   *"Countdown. No Act — "*
Sky's very absence talks. It says, 'Hang on there.'
>   *"Countdown. No — ·"*
I will hang on like rats at Coney Island,
Scrounging beady-eyed for popcorn under dumps.

> *"Count – "*
Give
Your spare minutes to my beggar bowl.
> *"Gate gate gate gate."*
This kleptomaniac clock. I sleepy, sleepy.
> *"Cliff-hanger, hush, let go."*

2. RE-INVENTING MAN AND –
I'm part of all that anywhere is sinking
It's me year's treadmill treads.
Look, I'm a tightrope's tightrope, veins pirouetting
On nerves. Both snapping.
Gravity plunks me on graves.
> *"The better to couple on, taunting the Reaper."*
I've been watching. You're suspiciously bulletproof
To the thermometer. You're Teflon to wrinkles.
Sneaking those pomegranates[10] in your bra,
With complicitous leers at crops,
You're still – admit it – goddessing around.
You said you'd stop. You're always at it, bedding
In green seedbeds, and then fall's red-light district.
> *"My job: to be clay's year-spin."*
The human job: to be clay's consciousness.

*   *   *

> *"Humans? I'm lodging a complaint about them at the gene bank.*
> *I'm returning for credit the ones I haven't used.*
> *They're just not user-friendly. When played with – "*
On second thought –
> *"Played with, they break."*
On second thought, I'd just as soon –
> *"Yet at YOUR gate I'll wait with – "*
I'd just as soon wait lone.
> *"I'll wait with you. An exception, just you. To share your*
> *Mortality, your throat's last rasp."*
Your errand-of-mercy I return unused.

---

[10] Persephone was caught eating that forbidden pomegranate after Hades.

Too busy ending this life-end poem,
My no to nothingness.
My futile no.

> *"Futile sweetened by the honesty of bitter.*
> *But earlier mortals said it all,*
> *And said forth gods."*

And unsaid them. True godliness? There's plenty
In hospices, reeking of urine, but not on Olympus.
True grace? I'll show you courage in cancer wards.
As for gods –

> *"I bet man toiled awful hard to invent us."*

Man re-invents man. Inventing gods was a cinch.

> *"What you can't 're' is death."*

I'm re-inventing not death but dying,
A knack gods lack. My hospital cot hones it.

> *"You write one poem and one poem only:*
> *The gallant human mess.*
> *There's self-destruct hubris when humans hump muses*
> *On a mattress off-limits to gods."*

Gods, we humans are a jealous people.
We worship graven images, engraved by
Pain, another knack you lack.
Pain plus brevity, making life
Keep re-inventing life.

> *"No Act Six."*

Were there more than Act Five, there'd be less.

3. AND SON OF MAN

> *"Don't tell the folks, but gods are atheists, and existence*
> *Needs non-existers. That's why folks value values."*

Now we, the veterans of pain, devalue
Unannealed gods.

> *"And what of the enigma of the valued?*
> *There was only one Christian. Not one of you understood.*
> *The water knew your carpenter had goat feet;*
> *He was dancing – not walking – on water.*
> *Sky enough for both crowns, the thorned and the vine-leaved.*
> *Our pagan feud with Christ? Mere ideology. Privately*

I would have brought him water on the hill.
That's when his man-clay was tested – was tempered –
Unendurably."
Annealed! And strewn Osiris, also annealed,
And hacked Dionysus and – and –
"The same, the same, and not quite the same.
Only the nailed one was doubly god. The miracle
Is in the mishmash, blending
A Pan who Found Out about pity
And a Jew-god drunk at last."
The carpenter's lips were dry; man wet them with wine.
Pan's eyes were dry; man wet them with tears.
Man's crisscross made god-halves whole.
"Miracle, yes, but retuning no winds.
From leaf to leaf the sun seeps down as before.
Blind rounds roll on. Blank coin rolls on.
All rolls and is and isn't.
Or – was there a ripple of swerve, a quick shrug of light,
In the circuits indifferent to man?
A blink of aware in their sleepwalk?"
I wish I knew.
I want to cry because I want to cry.
And because of how softly the moon silvers the treetops.
"The word you're fumbling for is 'poignant'."
Let's both shut up just a minute and hear small raindrops.

4. AMAZED TO CARE

"Back to business. What – now – of my year wheel?"
Now spins without you. Your nipples are brushing
No dust awake. Your ever-young unwrinkled
Hands stroke no buds.
Flower beds taunt you, 'Stick to Pluto's bed.'
Crops jeer, 'Look, we sprout solo.'
"Well, sure, eternal infinities don't last.
All gods were immortal.
Some poets will be."
Euphoria. Act Six.
"And some won't. For you no reprieve."

How can I tell when my gate comes knocking?
> *"Your throat rattling."*

And you? Can a godling outlast her last believer?
My de-shrined Kora and my decaying self,
We've shared quite a cycle of poems.
And now their end. And − like a kind
Hand over eyes − our end.
. . . Yet all's interweaving, though there is no weaver.
> *"Broken, you go for broke. Stripped now of pose, of props."*

Naked come, naked go.

* * *

> *"At land's end, where the sullen surf-slurp mumbles,*
> *We end Act Five. Same strand once more."*

Squashed dunes squish back. Ten thousand years of footprints,
Three-toed or five, sign here in vain.
The strand I pace, the sandglass of the sea,
Crumbles my time-grains while the wavelets tailgate
The waves and bump ashore.
> *"And throb your veins. There is no inland. Tide*
> *Is telling you something."*

I feel change near. Tide talking. Can't decode.
> *"Listen inside you."*

Can't pause. So much to finish. What's
This odd rattle?
Have I swallowed some toy? Lucky no rattlesnakes here.
Surely merely some baby's rattle.
Say 'yes' quick to confirm all's well.
> *"Amazed to care − I loving mere dust? − I bring you*
> *Tide's one kind wise reply:*
> *Honing − not hoping − more from ever less,*
> *Outdream the gate. Until it seeks you out."*

(1997-2000)

IV. NOT WORMS

(For Brodsky)

The night the poet died his metaphors
Gloated in liberation round his corpse.
Now rouged clichés, disguised as muse,
Ignite a bombing bombast's purple fuse.
Cant sneaks its Trojan Pegasus
Into Parnassus. Hoarse refugees race to warn us
That exclamation marks are running wild
And prowling half-truths carried off a child.
Fixed stars his vision etched into the skies
Now gouge – as falling stars – his too-wide eyes.
       Yet he throbs on in form to shatter
       This formless mutiny of matter.
       His dust is dead, his pulse a frightening thunder.
       Bell, book, and test tube can't exorcise its gong,
       Pulsing us into shapes of gargoyle wonder.
       In vain we drive our stakes through such a haunter.
       Are we but spilled iambics of his song?
       Are hearts feet lungs and couplings strummed
       By two-way thump,
       Scanning our outraged flesh with metric romp?
Yet some sereneness in our rage has guessed
That we are being blest and blest and blest
When least we know it and when coldest art
Seems hostile, useless, or apart.
Not worms, not worms in such a skull
But rhythms, rhythms writhe and sting and crawl.
They spin the seasons round from bud to snow.
And all things are because he tuned them so.

(March 2000)

PART III: Backtalk

NOW KINDNESS

I.

This was the summer when the tired girls
Breathed in the parks another planet's air
And stretched like hyphens between Here and There,
Stretched and lounged and sprawled on every lawn,
Each day a hammock cradling tired girls.
But then the planet of the tired girls
Spun from the constellation named The Fawn
(Goodbye, mild starlight of the Sign of Fawn)
And swung into the galaxy named Fangs,
Where from a tear-drop every dew-drop hangs.
This was the radiant pout of the withdrawn.
Who'd guess the sullen could be wise and valiant?
This was the gallant sulk of sullen girls.

II.

The ceremonious rite of budding girls:
With each new secret hair, with each disclosure,
The change, the Change creeps – by a hair-breadth – closer.
It's not just waves the moon's long tug unfurls.
For the first time in girlhood's carefree whirls,
Girls felt – through secret curls – moon's wounding reach.
Each felt the month's red message: "Grow up quick."
As if they *knew* of breasts, winds rippled tunic.
Mod casualness, umbilic to age-old lore.
A nervous tic, called "ripeness," the havoc of amor.
Panic, the branding-iron of gender's scar.
Wound that shall heal wounds, door not yet a door:
Is this the hub round which the whole earth twirls?
Commonplace – half mankind's – yet more, yet more. –
Commonplace and unique – creation's core:
Such riddles start when childhood ends for girls.

III.

The change said "doubt," said "trust no more." For girls,
Flamingos now were plastic, even when not.

Each "You" was an it, was a thing, each "who" a what.
Pet pearls, no matter how true, became glass pearls.

Then was the trusted nursery of Languish
(Goodbye, child's warming playroom-hearth of Languish)
Shrilled to the bad bad ecstasy of Anguish.
Serene old waltzing world (peace-ethics-laws)
Faded like sighs. Or begged like kitten paws.
Or soared, unheeded like a burnt-out star,
Into the limbo where the ambushed are
In this complicitous June of mussed up girls.

IV.
Then came the clouds of gnats that feed on girls,
Stalking and stinging through the gauze of dusk.
(Not even the art of Schiele and Lewis Carroll
Could shield young girls from feeling vulnerable.)
Then did all perfumes acridly take flight
Out of the satin cloying of Sweet Musk
(Goodbye, rich purring lassitudes of Musk
Dreamy anemias, yawns of dawdling girls)
Into the ache of spotlight named Take Fright.
Especially when they're unbreakable, toys break.
Then girls discovered that their dolls were dead,
Hollow yet lovely, like the gold skin shed
When locusts molt, discovered on trees by girls.

V.
If "brief" is what child-paradises cost,
Do Elementals reward what girls have lost?
Hard times reversed by soft discarded girls?
Peace ethics laws, only the fragile last.
Now kindness, wide-eyed as the dolls of girls,
Damaged and redeeming, shines from girls.

(2001 revised)

LINKS

I.

Sullen fog, befogging vision,
Making me throw rocks at sky.
What human links ungray my prison,
My fetter of frost? What warming tie
Can make ice cry?
Only ice, only tomb is sanitized. Wade
In green warm swamps of Mess before they're grayed.
What's left from ages righteous hate has scarred?
One poisoned dart.
From the scrubbed years of love's ethereal prayer?
One pubic hair.
Look, how things wilt at my touch. I'm the Midas of fade,
While older bones that ought to molder
Still rattle to sever my newer embraces.
Spooks with reproachful faces, winds with woman's voices,
Botched choices no Lethe erases,
All now compressed to one essence of unrest:
Gull lost on open seas.
When there's too much owing, nether
Worlds go seismic. Padlock cemeteries?
But what can I find to tether
The liquid graves of the drowned?
One gull plume's beached to haunt me,
A memo from those I disowned,
Those I wronged and those who wronged me,
They are linked to me by iced fetter.
. . . But fog, but fetter, both now shed,
Were mainly in our head.
And the they – now the "we" – in healing weather gather
In the fellowship of "we're fallible together."

II.

Next I proclaim a link of just us two.
Where, Deborah, is this autumn of me, of you

Heading? Frost? No, higher. One last fire
Is sparking what I've repressed in vain,
This outburst of clichés and outworn rhyme: –

> "I dreamed we drove down memory lane
> On a 'bicycle built for two' again
> As in the golden time, –
> Dove rhyming love, and rosebuds strewn like rain.
> It's then I discovered, as if brand-new,
> That roses are red and violets are blue.
> Such Hallmark bromides draw your boo,
> But this time trite is right."

Is rite of passage. Toward you, my youest you,
Your warm gate warming my western gate;
You my one past who hasn't passed, who danced
The tightrope of Whether, between late and too late;
Yes, you whose slim chin tilts against
The fog's grayed heather, you who – oh, who whatever.
I bring you – we, too, are beached – what had to fade,
What once could fly, this frayed feather.

(2000)

RHYTHMS OF PACINGS

(Two speakers, pacing Gethsemane's garden together: Jesus and then modem
man, the latter indented, in quotes, and in italics)

1. Garden Hour (gentle rhythms)

Toys don't know they're toys.
When you do, I ache.
Only one in twelve
Let me down. My self, my "Christian" self,
Broke twelve hundred thousand playthings
With loving fire and persuasive stake,
The spirit of "curse" Paul preached to the Galatians
Was not the spirit of the unthrown stone.
I loved God's toys with such a pure impatience
I loved them to death – improved them to death –
By purging the stain clay brings.
The fecund stain lashed back. Now dusk's gray wings
Descend. Leaves wilt at my breath.
Each palm that flung Palm Sunday flings
Ashes on my path.
Yet winds that scattered cremations
Are winds that scatter seed.
Sun-pulse to whom flesh prays,
Tilt me your lilting rays
That spilt on every weed but not my face.
I wanted warmth – men crammed me into creed.
Can I unsay what's said?
I hang around undead,
Gargoyle to every spire I ever built.
Around me children calling.
They dream I'll stop leaves falling.
I wear the rose of guilt.
> *"Wear pardon as a rose;*
> *We too, we playthings too,*
> *Make playthings wilt."*

84

* * *

Toys don't know they're toys.
> *"When we do, we wake.*
> *We rage we rage at what we know."*

That's half of one mistake.
I too, I tried to shake
My fist. Sky wouldn't quake.
No star fell out of step.
> *"A yes then?"* – Same mistake.
Accept acceptance so –
With somehow anyhow
A quiet no.

* * *

The hour in the garden,
The three days underground,
Changed me, made rage serene.
Remember all you felled
For heat or showman's sake?
The resin stuck around
After the logs were air
(As you will be) to make
The axe-hand smell of green.

2. Valse Macabre (raucous rhythms)

> *"Are we waltzers or waltz?"* – Both are trances
Between lap's hearth and grave's gloom.
> *"Must it be three-steps that dance us?"*
One two three, born breed and boom.
> *"Was the birth gate the best step or worst step?"*
Slide over, then under the loam.
> *"All gateways feel warm at the first step."*
All end in the same cold room.
> *"Whose dance band rules our start, our stop?"*
The traffic rhythm *is* the traffic cop.

*   *   *

     "Are we stepped by or stepping a three-step?"
One two three, root and uproot.
The rhythm your capering feet tap
Will soon tread your feet underfoot.
     "Womb-dark and tomb-dark are inkpots.
     Who writes? Are we author or plume?"
A life is a Rorschach of ink blots
Between an oom and an oom.

    3. Loam Hour (wistful rhythms)

     "Computing every tide,
     We calculate ebb and flow –
     And ask the dancers who dance us:
     Is it yes to the dance or no?"
Pressing clichés from roses,
Plodding slush from snow,
Best ask the loam that grows us:
What's down beyond yes and no?
     "You're not the only spark
     Went slumming in a tomb.
     There's not an oak missed three days under loam."
The grave's an acorn-launching trap.
     "From plummets summits; out of darkness comets."
Dark
My mother's lap.

    *   *   *

     "Gods eat their sons."
Each Sunday you eat God's.
     "Houdini Easter Lily,
     Jack in the box,
     You'll rise next April;
     Our coffin locks."

· Loam warms your noon – *"Just once."*

*   *   *

Once
Between exit and enter,
Between steps three and one,
You, the waltz's center,
Brush against sun.
> *"Globe-trotting Christmas tree*
> *Death-exempt tourist be advised:*
> *Hereabouts we're rationed on rebirth."*

As man I fall. As Christ I rise
To fall still more. – *"Then Easter lies?"*
The crown lied, not the thorns. The lilies
Must have been real: they festered.
> *"Dark twice is still our fare.*
> *Noon once and then where hide?"*

Acorns whom April Eastered
Toward axe and ember and air,
When twice what cloaks you closes,
Go down clear-eyed.

*   *   *

> *"Computing every tide,*
> *We calculate ebb and flow.*
> *Shall we ask the dancers who chose us*
> *If it's yes to the dance or no."*

Drowning where skulls are and seeds are,
Down beyond ebb and flow,
Go down in loam's dense ocean
With an affirming no.

(revised 2004)

DIALOGUE OF THE SCARS

(The two speakers are Christ and Everyman, the latter voice in quotes and italics)

1.

Now that Crucifixion and Holocaust
Are coffee-table books for a trendy host,
Take off a minute from aging to tell me how
It feels to grow up mortal. – *"Ow."*
So long since I went dying on my own.
How do you manage it? – *"Alone."*
I mean, what does it feel like? – *"Cold."*
Resist! Young rebels, how do *they* end? – *"Old."*
But ethics – brothers all. – *"Like Cain."*
Asylums needed. – *"For the sane."*
Man's load, I'll share it. – *"No such luck."*
I sold for thirty. – *"Lambchops for a buck."*
But I'm unique: I rose, I rose!
"One Lamb escaped the roast."
From me they made Wafers. – *"From later Jews soap."*
But Christians, being Christian, saved us. – *"Nope."*
But I'm Mr. Christian in person, not solely a Jew.
"Sure. By the way, Mr. Eichmann is looking for you."
Six million! Where can I find the memorial booth
For their lost golden dreams? – *"In a German gold tooth."*

2.

I tried to touch what's beyond the flesh.
"A beyond only flesh can touch."
Spirit and flesh, how mesh?
"Clutch."
I threw no stones at any Mary M.
"Your fans throw them."
I wore thorns. – *"They don't."*
Why am I owned by all I once disowned?
"Why does 'pray' sound like 'prey'?"
I lugged a cross uphill once. Say
If you have. – *"Nine to five each day."*

Who else blooms Easter back with April showers?
"All funeral parlors 'say it with flowers'."
And while the nails – and when the gall –
My parents – why didn't they help at all?
"Whose really do?"
My father wouldn't stop the spear. – *"Same here."*
O mother, I'd hoped it wouldn't hurt. – *"Me too."*

(revised 1995-1999)

DIALOGUE OF THE BANGS

(The speakers are God and Everyman, the latter in quotes and italics.)

God's Big Bang: creation. Infinite mass.
     "Man's wee bang: mutation. Brief new cosmos."
Macro, micro. – *"Cat, mouse?"*
Galactic Order versus fluke-gene mess.
Repose versus gamut. Mortal gamut of vile
And would-be sublime. Meanwhile
I'm stainless – and scarless – forever. – *"Gods*
     Are dime a dozen. Against all odds
     One wakening ow-uniqueness
     Utters the all of is, its yes,
     Its no. And then goes bust."
Eternity, so famous for being famous, –
     "Sleeps dark. What shines is fluke-spark.
     Its name – " – Don't name it! – *"MY name is – "*
Biped dust-heap? – *"Conscious dust."*

(1999)

LOOKING AROUND

There was this water. Noon's
Ray on an oil spill – a palette of tints.
Then a phantom voice (don't label) where the breakwater ends:
"What's wrong with god-creeds is not that they don't make sense
But that they're not crazy enough. Look around for once."

*   *   *

Where the breakwater ends,
What floods towards me at ocean's stone-boned fence?
Where breaker meets breakwater's No and bends,
Is there a golden surfboard, tugged by swans,
Or a Venus birth that a shark rends?
Where the breakwater ends,
A pair of empty phantom shoes (don't label in advance:
The drowner might be you or me a decade hence)
Descends.

*   *   *

Wasn't there once
A graffito "to the unknown god" in Athens?
I've been looking around: from Big Bang to jumpy electrons,
He out-impossibles our most impossible superstitions,
He, the Creator I'm still creating ever since
The ray, the oil, the sea's fence.

(1995-1998)

PRIMO LEVI [11]

Where's home? From Auschwitz homeward came
A chemist with a Jewish name.
He saw, he wrote. Truth's words remain.
Sights driving other men insane
Had left him seemingly urbane
As if truth's tears were a cleansing rain
   For pain and stain.

But he, unbearably alone,
He the surviving, homeward one,
Decoding all chemicals but the dome
Of unsolved gray behind skull's bone
(He tugged downward by his own
Home-coming up the stairs from hell),
He from his own home stairwell
   Fell.

      (1999)

---

[11] Apparently committed suicide (having written the definitive Auschwitz memoir) down his high stairwell.

WHEN STORMS REPLACE BREEZES

1.

If blossoms could blossom
One petal of petals
To whom all other blooms are
As leaves are to flowers,
It would be to the others
As you are, my daughter,
To all other daughters
Whom songs are adorning.
For what am I here for
If not to make love-songs
Of all the world's beauty
Whose birthday we share?

2.

If subtlest of fragrances
Brewed a quintessence
Too delicate-pure
To ever be breathed,
It would be to the others
As you are, my daughter,
To all other daughters
Whom songs are encircling.
For what am I here for
If not to weave lassos
Of song for the lonely
To tug them to love?

3.

Say yes to the breezes;
If any dishevels
One curl of a ringlet,
I'll know and be with you.
The grace-notes that feather
The wing-beats of longing
Are lead till they heal with
Their singing your crying.

For what is a song for
If not to smooth ringlets
Of daughters too hurt by
The prose of the world?

4.

When storms replace breezes,
No hurt can have healing.
Then the love I now sing you
Can pillow your fading.
For what am I here for
If not to link fingers
With daughters whose wistfulness
Worlds never answer?
For what is a song for
If not to stretch hands out
To signal the falling,
"You're never alone"?

5.

When the camp says: "Dig graves now,
We're coming to shoot you,"
I'll help with your shovel
– (I'll know and be with you) –
To give you more seconds
To look up from digging
To look at the sun while
I pillow the sand out.
For what is love here for
If not to smooth ditches
For all the world's daughters
Whose dying we share?

(Revised 2003) (Written 1945)

WONDERING

(to Anya)

When both are strong with tenderness, too wild
With oneness to be severance-reconciled:
When even the touch of fingertips can shock
Both to such seesaw mutuality
Of hot-pressed opposites as smelts a tree
Tighter to its dryad than to its own tight bark;
When neither jokes or mopes or hates alone
Or wakes untangled from the other; when
More-warm-than-soul, more-deep-than-gut are one
In marriage of the very skeleton; –

When, then, soil peels the flesh off half this love
And locks it from the unstripped half above,
Who's ever sure which side of soil he's on?
Have I lain seconds here, or years like this?
I'm sure of nothing else but loneliness
And darkness. Here's such black as stuffs a tomb,
Or merely midnight in an unshared room.
Holding my breath for fear my breath is gone,
Unmoving and afraid to try to move,
Knowing only you have somehow left my side.

I lie here, wondering which of us has died.

(revised 2004)

94

(These levels are geographic [sky, earth], godly [Father Ouranos, Mother Gaea], and bodily [word rhythms imitating the pair's contrasting erotic rhythms].)

I. Autumn Serenade: Sky to Earth

If through a wind I ripple every tide
With such a wave as rattles every quay,
It is to haunt the true lost flesh they hide;
All sea, all soil but sheathe my bride from me.

Her skirt of colored seasons crowns her thighs
And circles round the lunar tune she sways.
– O loose your sweet green locks with drowsy grace
And slowly brush their warmth across my eyes.

Twisting your shoulder-blades beneath the plough
That fondles you when apple twigs are bent,
Deep in your hills you would not huddle so
If you believed how sad I am you went.

Then let no princeling of the apricots
Excite you with the ripeness of the year.
His nectared cheeks must burst; your courtier rots;
My snows are on his trail, will soon be here.

And yet am sun. I nibble listlessly
A ghaut[12] of all the wives of all my whims.
Autumnal tawny harems burn for me.
Such games will not distract me from your limbs.

Call to me dawdlingly when summer falters.
Attract me bitterly through molten grain.
I am your sky; look up; my clouds are altars
To worship you with desecrating rain.

---

[12] A burning ghaut, like autumn's reddening leaves, is the funeral pyre on which the widows of a Hindu prince were traditionally burnt.

II. Counter-Serenade: She Invokes the Autumn Instant

Then touch the park; the leaves are stained to lure you.
The leaves are spread on winds they fan befóre you.
They drained the summer, and their veins prefér you,
Dark with the season they are keening for.

Then bring the heavy dying they prefer.
Each painful fruit is hanging heavier.
Why pause when loveliness grows lonelier
And love is just as melting as it looks?
There's but one touch that all the ripeness lacks:
You are the instant; you are waited for.

Then never wait when flutes of foliage bear you
Home on the homeward tune they always bore.
Fear not at all the twigs of flame they bear.
These never meant to be a barrier.
The lovely are as lonely as their gleam,
The lonely just as loving as they seem,
The fruits as melting as they always were:
There is a fondling they are furtive for.

Then touch my park. The leaves have spread befóre you
The green they drained, the darkness they prefer.
Come to the leaves, reach out and touch them all.
Bring to the smoldering year, that hovers fór you,
The hovering instant love is dawdling for:

There's not one leaf that does not long to fall.

(revised 1995-2000)

RITES

Up from primordial past,
As long as time holds fast,
Two jigsaw puzzles last
Unsolved (gene's trap? Or nest?).
They're what we all know best
And understand the least.
The powers of atom and sun we've leased;
These inches of flesh we've never leashed;
It's us their ritual lashed.
Her crescent round his crest,
Child's mouth around her breast,
She port for either unrest:
Two tempests stunned by rest.

(2000)

SOLE SPEAKER: Pluto. Why the "hell" shouldn't he be Pluto? Isn't the universe surreal enough for this? Or is he instead – or in addition – the basement janitor of an American apartment house? Has a brain tumor made him think he is brother of Zeus and god of the Greek underworld?

TIME: Spring. His girlfriend Persie has just deserted him a half-year for Dion, a wine-salesman poet on top floor of same building.

PLACE: A hospital dissection table, where – in a tumor autopsy – dead brain cells are galvanized awake for an instant by the surgeon-scalpel. Though the whole resultant Pluto monologue flashes by in that instant, the instant seems a million-year reign to the knife-sparked cells.

MYTHOS: Found in hospital libraries and read there by speaker, Bullfinch's *Mythology* has somewhat crudely popularized the familiar legend of Pluto and Persephone. After being kidnapped while gathering flowers at Enna, she forfeits any permanent return by her forbidden pomegranate nibble. Thereafter she shuttles. In spring: regreener of earth and of the wine god Dionysus-Bacchus-"Zagreus" (Greek for "the hacked"). In winter: Pluto's queen. Their watchdog: three-headed Cerberus. Their flower: asphodel. Their rivers: the Lethe of forgetfulness and the Styx of Charon, the obol-fee ferryman.

INDENTATION: Whenever speaker becomes aware of his human janitorial self.

I.

I.D. card: Greek and Roman made Hades my cognomen,
A.k.a. Dis or Pluto.
I'm act five, sparing no man. At Enna of ill omen,
I dragged me a bobby-sox goddess below,
A flower child then. She's a swinger now
As emcee of Dion, my foeman.

Before they swing too heated on vineyard's fertile seedbed,
Tell wine tout and his woman: if they commit the seed-spread
Perversion called life, with obscene plant or human,
They'll catch the plague called green.
Man's chromosomes know if death hadn't weeded
Hug's garden, they'd still (ask Darwin) be bugs.

* * *

But octopoding upward through my freeze,
What sinister green tentacles are these,
Strangling the fields I'd freed from the life disease?
Sleazy rouged roses have turned on the spigots
Of spring propaganda for anti-death bigots.
What right have the bigots to get so polemical?
Am I accountable to some biodegradable chemical?
Mortality isn't popular with mortals.
They curse, they pray — I answer both with chortles.
They spurn (are they sick or mad?) a wholesome
Necrophilia. I'm broad-minded, but my portals
Allow no vitaphiles. They're just too loathsome.
The erotic being their most addictive narcotic,
Birth is their itchiest venereal infection,
Cured (over the counter, you need no prescription)
By a dose of antibiotic named Thanatos.
Call life — bed being where it's relayed —
A bedbug. A dandy cure is: squash it.
Or feed it prussic acid. Or just gas it.
I purify. Pure means BLANK SLATE.
Even for sky. My net's entropic strands
Scoop up all stars, these falling sandglass sands.

* * *

Alcoholic of diabolic, I can't stop swigging doom.
Yet for beauty I'll always stop, panting with joy:
A sleek hearse, a cute shark, an intense bomb,
A well-crafted torture toy.
My tombs have panache worth dying for:
A user-friendly sepulcher.

Nineteenth-century deaths had style, two gems my best:
1821, John's writ-in-water jest;
1865, Abe's slow train west.
Why do the dying wrong me so,
As if I'm some feelingless juggernaut plow?
Tearing off wings or as urn's decorator,
I, not they, am the sensitive creator.
A bad press on funerals gets under my skin.
Humph, every one but me's a philistine.
I wish tamed wilds would spawn one untamed faun,
Even a mangy louse-nipped one,
To sign my ugh at what apes uglify.
Ho hum, I've outlasted so many eternities;
Each time, when nothing's left, not even zero,
This 'nothing' barfs a new big bang and – presto –
New galaxies.

*　　*　　*

Or am I a corpse hallucinating all this?
Dead brain re-sparked by my dissector's gashes?
Waking a cell's last ember? Tickled ashes?
A recharged battery's accidental sputter?
My Pluto years only one second as true time is reckoned?
(My only Greek the myth book on my cot?)
No, no; the lies apes mutter
Can't break my royal rod.
Nor can the tricks of her upstart grape-shill god.
Let him go back to Asia and take back
The grotesque alcohol-berries he tries to hawk.
(Name him? I wouldn't condescend.)
Dissectors can shred me to bits; what they can't do is kill me
So long as I say – no, screech – as the blades descend,
"I'm not human. You're slashing quicksand."
Me die? As death's boss, how can I? Reality
Is what I tell it to be. As number-one god,
I'm at peace with my lot. – O why am I really not?
O why? Too proud to admit it near my throne,
Even a night god needs personal noon:

HER homecoming footsteps traipsing down,
Hair still half-bleached from sun.
Here come my courtiers (boneyard, basalt, fossils)
To polish apples – I mean asphodels.
Ah, how they bore me when she's gone.
Here come my harems (lamias, lemurs, snow
Maidens). How I miss my one no-show.
Go-to-hell is the prettiest banner ever unfurled;
I wish she would.
Devil-take-her: my favorite blessing in all the world;
I wish I could.
I'd kidnapped me a bimbo. I spread her limbs akimbo.
Her limbs then kidnapped me. And left. I'm left in limbo.

    My gray cells twitch. What jabs my gray?
    And what high glare beats down?
    Is it doc's flashlight? No, call it the sun
    She smuggled down when I said gods need noon.
    Reality isn't the worlds of outside clay.
    Reality is in my gray.

       II.

Nine lackeys I gave her (more than her wino spared):
Three darling furry imps kept her coiffeured;
Three demons poured the poppy juice we shared
Before three more prepared the nuptial grave.
Because my dank cave, cozy as a bier,
Lacks music for her music-craving ear,
I xylophoned my stalactite chandelier.
Because her art-of-love out-Ovids Ovid,
I gave her anklets pluto-crats would covet
(My own hands snapped them on) of solid gold.
Because her waist is graceful to behold,
I wove – to make our link endure –
A girdle of fragrant toadstools, dainty mold,
And skulls my worms scrubbed pure.
Because she likes cruel laughs, I used to spoof
Each shade below for his worst goof:
That cad Achilles for the heel he hid
In jackboot swagger; Troy for the wooden steed

That was also a mole; a cuckold kinglet for
A runaway wife who started a war;
Orph for his bungled rescue tour;
Poor Jason for the ill-advised idea
Of letting his baby-sitter be Medea;
Two sons, O. and O. (each did a parent in),[13]
For a sin – or call it hangup – Furies haunt.
Hell hath no woman like a Fury scorned.

     *   *   *

Because on buried night-like days
She whined about frostbite and wheedled for blaze,
I crushed – with my eons and with my tons –
Ferns into hibernating arsons
Called coals, these volcanoes of substitute sunrays,
Whose cold black woke into comfy red instead.
Who cares if my Etnas arsoned a dozen ape towns above,
So long as my love got her fireplace?
Do apes care? But they're clods, not gods; her laurels
For ape bards have engendered our worst quarrels.
Why can't she have decent values? – pride, will, and cruelty?
I taught her ruthlessness; whom did she use it on? Me.
While I lectured her on 'evil, be thou my good,'
She got so bored she snored. Which shocked me morally.
Didn't I do – to keep her – all I could?
My bedside Bullfinch taught me what's her food;
I had my Borgia chef whip up soufflés
Of pomegranates; they won mere half-year stays.
I buttered up Ceres, her mother; but Persie sneaked away,
Planting vile vines with her lover, subverting my Law of Decay.
Tell word-tout Dion and his groupies, with their yen
(As if it were their dildo) for his pen, –
Tell them I spot a phony every time.
Am I jealous? You bet! Hell makes punishment fit the crime
(Ask Tantalus), and I'll sentence him to rhyme
Forever, – understood never.

---

[13] Oedipus and Orestes

III.

My giant poise isn't embarrassed emoting on Richter scale eight,
Quaking the earth with my hate as once with my joys.
(If that's too bombastic for pygmies, let 'em sneer prissily.)
    In the patients' – no, prisoners' – library,
    That's where I boned up on Persephone
    After they lugged me through hospital doors,
    Calling my royal dreams plebeian tumors.
    Or if I'm no god, the more dignity
    To my stubborn "I am that I am."
    Must I ham an emperor Elba'd in janitor slacks?
    More hacked by gibes than vine by ax,
    I join the *noblesse* of the demeaned. Storm whacks
    Me worse than it did Lear – with panics worse than Mac's
    When he was facing Birnam's woodsy nooks.
    Anachro? Can I, a B.C. Hellene, wax
    So Shakespearean? Ah, those hospital books.
    They'd even make – take a random example – mere janitors
    Talk in pentameters.
Roaches fill basement cracks. Greek gods, de-shrined
By men, in turn de-shrine mankind
By infesting the cracked basements of the mind.
Like roaches, we scatter when lights are shined,
Leaving only – for pedants and poets to find –
Contemptuous droppings behind.
    Whatever outraged topside, here gets staged.
    I'd rather sulk in a basement than abasement.
    "Janitor" almost sounds like "genital,"
    The under-the-belt of global.
    When tenants, not guessing how soon they'll owe an obol,
    Flush gallons of sewage down at me, when they
    Yell for more heat (they'll get their fill in hell),
    I'll send a cobra up their pipes one day
    Or stuff the boiler with dynamite and blow
    The whole smug building up.
    Down here, all signs point down, not up.
    A janitor knows the respectable from below.
    They'll be sorry, they'll be sorry,

That grape-crazed top-floor pair belittling me.
While she's pawed giggly-wiggly by his passes,
Must I slave at stoking coal to warm the asses
Of those who, when they're Styxed, must slave for me?

      IV.
Brer Zeus yanked a girl from a migraine.
(None called Athena his tumor.)
Me too? Is the sharp kiss jabbing my brain
The girl I'm horny for?
    "Sharp kiss": the words save me. Here I slough
    (She's back!) my exile off – and resume my reign,
    Freed from my coal-stoke years. But the scalpel-sharp pain
    Keeps on. I'm feeling what humans must feel –
    If it's true, what I've heard, that they're able to feel.
    (Silent voice shouting from fringe of my brain:
    "FOOTSORE AND VERY LONG IS THE SHORT HUMAN
    LANE.")
Is she back? Did she miss – in spring's green jail –
Winters when nobly fungus-pale
We ruled together on black obsidian thrones?
Palace of blackness: charcoal, crows,
Petits-fours coffins stacked as dominoes.
Lamps: lit with lard of emperors and priests.
Walls richly draped: with pelts of the ape beasts.
Persephone herself each winter dead,
The Cleopatra of the carrions.
Each winter, rushing to my arms, her bones –
Like molting snakes – would shed
Her flesh with a sassy striptease twist.
With a final shake as catalyst,
Snapping life's last bind like a thread,
The rind – strip, strip – the rind, the rind has fled,
Outnuding nakedness. The terrible barrenness
Of her crescent cicatrix –
Cold as the moon it's no more bleeding for –
Now blooms forth more delirium down here
Than when some topside Venus ungirdles her

Warm Venus-flytrap calyx.
The graduates of my graves have appetites
Grosser than airy ghosts, than tacky sprites.
Pounding peeled bones, not flesh-guck, on the Styx,
We get our kicks from skeletons,
Frictions more penetrant than skin-deep pounce,
More intimate than pneumatic bounce.
My dead give "small deaths" to my dead.
    (Or it this just a lurid wet
      Dream on a janitor's lone bed?)
I don't know why "jab," so artistic-sadistic
A verb, keeps haunting my fevers.
I dote on my scepter-jabbing trick
Of electroshocking the dead, click click,
Into capering cadavers.
As if they've Parkinson's, each of my dead
(Lively, not living: a corpse with a nervous tic)
Quivers. As if from tarantula's terpsichorean bite.
Crunching like popcorn under my boot,
Their dancing toes rot off, are strewn about,
As if they're lepers gone spastic.
    (As if? As if? When I stretch the surreal, the fabric
      Rips its elastic.)
"Delirium blooms," I said. My dead go mad
With lust, hate, hunger. They self-destruct, they shred
Each other's sockets, they gnaw their own
Tibias, leaving a garbage of bone
To fertilize spring's picnic.
This is how winters end. But up to then,
Picture us two, our most idyllic scene:
Both throned; my pet bat on my wrist;
She giving Cerberus's heads a pat,
His gruff arf more mellifluous to my ear
Than birds of her wino's bards. (I'd cheer
If in his eye some hailed-blithe-spirit pissed.)

V.

She and I: too late to repair rapport?
O isn't it enough that once we were
This much to me, that much to her?
Am I no more to her or she to me
Than cast-off condoms floating down the Lethe?
Did she hold back the tears she should have shed?
Why didn't she say the word she never said?
My airborne satellites, the vultures, say
Plenty. They photo'd her today
Red-handed with roses and guilty of clay.
With ticklings called ripe, she shocks blueberries blue
And titillates pears to blush a pinker hue.
His vineyards excite her orgiastic japes;
Shameless with Bacchic fun,
She gulps ejaculating body fluids from
Grapes.

* * *

What price her treasons? What got sold out to whom?
Each time she corpsed six months, I used to groom
Her skeleton squeaky clean. But now it wears
The rags of squish called meat.
With the drug called grow, she spreads the contagion called wheat
And openly hobnobs with the freaks upstairs,
Those monsters who dung and couple on the soil
They'll soon be under. For this, she sold her sweet
Treasure, her infernal soul.

VI.

Rumor: all's one big tidal melody,
Twining not two motifs but three, –
My ebb, his ebb, her sea. Two shores, one flow.
Well, I won't have it so.
No infra-dig *ménage-a-trois*. She'll cling –
After tonight – for keeps to the true king.
Flunkies, fetch me my magic scything wand.
Tonight I slam my holy-murder hand

On tide, on seasons, her year wheel, the balanced
Seesaw of for and against.
She's priestess of balance. I want it all ice, and he
Wants life's insolent evergreen poetry.
Recidivist life just can't keep on recycling
(Spurting and burying, buried and re-spurting)
The seed pus of its running sore.
Some day life can't go Eastering any more.
I'll end this damned green leprosy.
When her Dion-Zagreus-Osiris is hacked by my just scythe;
Stretched out as protein for crows,
What flows is not her metronoming sea
But grape's swart gore.
Convulsed like a fish-hooked worm on the floor,
Under the bed where they once were blithe,
Let his crybaby-sidekick sob and writhe
(Till her lids and her lobes are red)
For the vine god dead on the vineyard snow.
I veto what I veto.

   *   *   *

A millennium later – or was it ago? –
Her wheel hasn't stopped for his yes or my no.
We both thought we're brakes; we're spokes.
My dead don't stay dead, his quick don't stay quick.
Three rival roles; apart, we're three sick jokes;
Joined, an impossible
Harmony, making everything possible.
    A trillion everythings from three?
    Impossible. And what if reality asks
    Whether I've merely a janitor's I.D.?
    – It doesn't matter. Changing our names, our masks
    But never our three relentless tasks,
    We non-existers make existence be.

VII.

Kind dusk and gentle reverie.
A grandma fabling for children.
This is the ancient tale of the three.
This is the future tale of the trillion.
The children, bored (they'd rather play soccer).
Retell is blurred, with new myth garnished.
Smelling of urine and roses, clasping a nursing-home garland,
Alzheimer'd granny is fabling on her rocker:
Tales truer for being garbled.
Is it she who rocks earth around sun?
Has she unwittingly gardened
March? Frost garbaged? Wheel guarded?
A dingy hospice, unknown
To our trio; yet wheel's secret hub.

Afar in a pub – for a swig, for a puff –
Some village Homer tells some village oaf
The tale of how the three,
Each to our own rite true,
Each trapped in the same comic tragedy,
Did what each had to do.

(End of voice from below, whatever its source. The dissecting scalpel has now been withdrawn from its instant of poke and wiped clean of messy brain cells)

(revised 1998)

UNTHINGS

Come stay with what can't stay.
Trust only what fades away.
Skies wish they'd made us button-eyed.
In autumn only man is heavy-eyed.
Such eyes: sky-storming wings.
We first don't know we're things.
When we do, we're not.
When we're not, we wake as rings:
A circle, not a dot.
Are we a sick gene's blunder?
Call us the unthing wonder.

*   *   *

Go leave with what's not staying.
Trust only the ebb-half of seas.
Singing is not quite fading.
Euterpe. Euphonies.
Autumn's not quite my opponent.
We are and aren't things.
An eon must echo a moment
When a moment has resonant strings.
I'm going to exit sonant,
A harp-nerve strummed by a breeze.

(1999)

I. BACKTALK TO SKY

– But close as handclasps before surgery,
Brief warmth outlasts mere cold eternity.
(Diamond voice in man's soft pate:
"I am the hardness called 'create'.")
The weight that crushes out of coals
The density of diamonds, rolls
Lighter than how intolerable pressures cram
Our briefness in the lastingness called "Form."
(Coal voice: "No lastings. Only weight.")

* * *

Intense as loneness in failed surgery,
Botched dreams outlive mere immortality
And hurt us into massacres and beauty.
We failures, botched by a God that fails,
Are garbage bags of brine and follies,
A garbage that feels.
We can't transcend our curtains' falls;
Creed's bootstrap-lift feels false.
We're literally God-damned fools –
But a bit more than trash for landfills.
What is it, this "bit" of frills:
A rogue-gene fluke that bullies god? – or will's
Clenched fist that wilts?
Don't crown us garbage bags with thorns – with laurels –
But with a cap of bells.

* * *

We are a Jealous People when ignored.
Our "graven images" outlord our Lord.
They heckle (it's a cosmic scandal)
Entropy. Yes, briefly. Yet
. Oh shiningest when terminal.
Free will? Our tiny bit of it,

Only one spilled dab,
Spoiled the whole test tube in the sky lab.
Transfiguring the end we can't transcend,
Here is our graven Here, our intimate own:
A sere leaf hanging warmly on
A bit till down.

*   *   *

    Sky voice:
    "This time the guck I mold got out of
    Hand. Next planet no souls."

(1998)

II. EARTH VOICE

(Eve talking back to Up There)

Numb Boss who calls empathy girlish, I call the stars you twirl forth
Cogs, not growth.
I call your atoms – till bounded by my dense finiteness –
Infinite froth.
Lonesome up there? Is this why your pawing winters undress
Green-smocked earth?

Your eons, they're ogling my hour – they ache for my April caress,
Recharging the warmth
Drained from your cosmos: Like Boaz[14] must cold foot Entropy
       press
A hot-water bottle named Ruth?
Evolution presents her new baby, nicknamed "God's Image;" come
       bless
Amoeba's aftermath;

---

[14] Rewarming of patriarch Boaz, cf. Book of Ruth, 3, 7, 14: "And she came
softly, and uncovered her feet and laid her down . . . And she lay at his feet
until the morning."

"Flush it down the toilet, it's human," you chuckle benignly. "Why
        nurse
Ape's afterbirth?" . . .
Turning swine into men by casting them pearls, I reverse
Circe myth.
"What does woman want?" Not be – at flaming hearth –
Moth.

Albino God, patron of fungus, your envy of birth-force
Forced birth pangs on birth.
Squeamish butcher. I bleed – and even your bloodbaths can't face
Witch broth;
Gag, barren sky, on my tribute of monthly yes
To loam-truth.

Hygienic busybody, must you clean up loam's mess?
Must root eke wrath?
All night, all night, poor perfect God, your deathless
Pure breath
Stinks – like deodorized "underarm daintiness" –
Deader than death.

(1987-1998)

EXULT?

I can't get home out here.
My world hangs by a hair.
The "out" for which I sighed
(The secret exit back to home)
       Is not outside.

   *   *   *

Compass and doctor warned
Of west, of heart arrest.
Shade blots the lawn I want
And blots my — let's forget the rest.
Gnawing my heart, what parasite?
I'm tired of being tired. At reaper's scythe
       I merely yawn.

   *   *   *

"Don't think you're so special," says lawn.
"Same west for everyone.
Your night's just any night
That hangs around for dawn."
—   No dawn-rise. Down is down.
Circle's a one-way ring.
Amor, beauty, song
Melt toward oblivion.
Yet . . . I'm an icicle shining
       An instant with sun.

   *   *   *

Sage geezer? Not my thing.
Uplift? Not in sight.
Rather Catullus, down in loam,
Than crest of Everest.
But my worn verse can't hone;
Bleak insights can't incite.
Shade gulps down lawn by lawn.

Leaf, with its broken wrist,
  Can't cling.

  *   *   *

But do I want to cling?
I'm owned by what I own.
I used to want more lawn.
I used to want to want.
        But will has waned.

  *   *   *

Compass and doc, be warned:
I'll stash in house arrest
The old self at my side.
The unrest of "I want"
I'll shove aside. I'll wrest —
From wound — a magic wand.
I am my old self's heir.
The growth of grass is what I hear
Now that I'm deaf to lawn.
Earth voice? I'm nearer her
Now that home waits in bone.
I would exult, but wonder locks my breast.
        Here isn't here.

  *   *   *

A fall is not a wing;
West shade is not east light.
Yet when the two collide,
Wilted can mean caressed.
Are light and shade allied?
Reversing cycle's swing,
My belly wallows in the grass I hear,
The mulch I'm from, the mulch where I'll reside,
        Creation's site.

*   *   *

This moment will decide.
Some change is in the air.
Heart pounding wild delight,
Am I about to sing?
    –   An end's a kind of rest.
A rest's a kind of home.
I'm going – rest is here –
        Home inside.   (1999)

WHICH FIRST?
"I've first an intention, and then I enact it."
Intent's invented after you've acted.

OOPS
I've swallowed the poison, changed my mind, and there's no phone.
What do I do next if I'm alone?

NOTHING'S UNACCIDENTAL
"How can we tell our fate from coincidence?"
We askers, we ourselves are accidents.

CREATOR WITH NO CAPITAL "C"
"Aren't we meaningless flukes without a Sky-cop on duty?"
Our job as brief flukes: eke beauty from flukey.

PANTHEISM
"There are no gods." – Hooray.
"We all are gods." – Oy veh.

EPPUR MUOVE
Emperor Julian Apostate, "Vicisti, Galilei."
Church to science, "Vicisti, Galileo."

ST. FRANCIS, PRE-INQUISITION
They made me this fancy rich dome I didn't want them to make.
Three hundred years later they would have made me a stake.

MOTHER TERESA
Her "sainthood"? – cardinals quibble. Meanwhile Calcutta glows
With light a thousand saints could not impose.

EVE
I was always in secret the Foamborn, goddessing through
Shrines, plus smut on walls of loo.

TO EVE, DE PROFUNDIS
Launch us beyond the flesh, bow of lap's arch,
To beyonds only flesh can reach.

HER BEYONDS
For insecure males, beyonds are too demanding a test.
Hence Macho, the Taliban beard of the west.

CHRIST TO ANTI-CHRIST
Nietzsche, my thorn-crowned brother, why do you wrong me so?
Give me your hand. I was always . . . Dionysus-Bromio.

SAME DIALOGUE (NIETZSCHE, NAZARENE)
"Our crowns? Not thorns but clown bells."
And, at last, laurels.

HALVES
"Can we glimpse the heavenly city?" – Not till both gods join
              hands:
Pan finding out about pity, and the Pale One in drunken dance.

WHAT WE ARE IS –
– Earth's bellyache. What we think we are is Faustus.
Death is the peristalsis that ousts us.

UNDERGROUND MOVEMENT
"Saint Paul mugged Venus. She couldn't rebound."
But changing into vice, went underground.

VENUSBERG REBOUNDING
"What's left of her? A soured neurosis?"
Tannhaüser's staff flowered new roses.

MY FRIEND'S METASTASIZED CERVIX CANCER
Her wound; her courage while Crab multiplied;
The one-eyed stare defying the Argus-eyed.

DEEP-SEATED GRIEVANCE
"Old age with dignity." – Cant of a fool.
Odds are you'll die straining at stool.

NOT WORTH IT
To end as clay. Overpriced. Who'll repay
My million deaths of aching evolvings, up from clay.

BUT LIFE GOES ON: WORTH IT ANYHOW?
Life, come to me, glass in hand; ass in skirt;
Sassy-voiced; moist.

FOAMBORN MISCHIEF
O what is "heart" that we fumble when we feel?
"Mother. I cannot mind my wheel."[15]

OVERPOPULATED
"Completely empty, completely crowded town?"
You're not alone in being all alone.

THE THUDDINGNESS OF FRUITS
Soil – Sesame – you let me out last spring.
This time – knock, knock – let me in.

"HANG IN THERE"
Weight of that season. Wan crown
Of leaves. Unburden? Down.

DEAR READER, GOODBYE
Look. That leaf.
It falls with relief.

---

[15] One line from Sappho fragment.

My 89th Year

"I polish spittoons for God." – *Langston Hughes*

I. Years

The years, the years, they weigh me down,
Too heavy to be heaved by me.
Time's sentence is imposed on me.
It cannot be reprieved by me.
"They flee from me who sometime did me seek,"
Readers who'd been close cleaved to me.
I have grand plans for books to write.
They cannot be achieved by me.
My favorite-friends – Dwight, Van – are dead.
What grief can next be grieved by me?
No guru's mine, and no divine
Belief can be believed by me –
Except the Athens "Unknown God."
It's He can be perceived by me.
It's He commands, "Thou shalt not sneak."
No more tricks up-sleaved by me.
I've tangled up my life's botched web
Too long to be reweaved by me.
I want my kids, I want two more.
Kids now can't be conceived by me.
I have no steno, no home help,
No butler to be Jeeved by me.
And if I asked my neighbors' help,
I know how they'd be peeved by me.
I am un-Edened Adam
With no mate to be Eve'd by me.
I lust to steal more hearts for lust.
They cannot be re-thieved by me.
No light is light enough to light
The arrow-lights once sheaved by me.

II. Metamorphs

My tree's gouged bare by winter claws.
It cannot be re-leaved by me.
Too late to be relieved by me.
Though I've probed wombs to feel reborn,
Birth's innocence can't be relived by me.
Yet gloved hands can't be laved by me.
Only stain unstains. Soiled soil
Keeps white the white birch loved by me.
Caterpillar, moth. What strange adult is
Larva'd by me?

III. Acorns

Lost pasts can't be retrieved by me.
Though hope can't be received by me,
I've got this far without.
Shan't chill young hopers with my doubt.
Of "wow!" they're not bereaved by me.
Death is the one I scheme to rout.
He cannot be deceived by me.

*   *   *

What's left of me when life is out?
Acorned rhymes. Sprout?

(2005)

120

PART IV: Transplantings

A few samples from the author's unpublished
book manuscript, entitled:

*Transplantings: Goethe, Stefan George, and Georg Heym,
Englished and Analyzed, With Reflections on Modern German
Poetry and the Art of Translation*

THREE POEMS BY GEORG HEYM

(awarded the Columbia University Translation Grant) (written 2000)

1987 was the hundredth anniversary of the birth of Georg Heym (1887-1912). It deserved to be an occasion for celebration. It wasn't, not in America. No book of his has appeared in the English-speaking world, where this major poet is still little known. An aesthetically and politically radical co-founder of the German "Expressionist" movement, Heym died by drowning in a skating accident at the age of 24. His early poems are mostly worthless and imitative juvenilia. The poems written during the months before his early death are among the most original in the twentieth century and today surprisingly "modern." First forgotten, then rediscovered (after World War II seemed to justify his desperate predictions of doom), Heym has become a leading influence on German literature today.

These "transplantings" from Heym (like those by me from Stefan George in the September 1987 issue of *Parnassus)* are excerpts from my unpublished book of translations and essays about translation: *Double Star: The Oscillating Orbits of Stefan George and Georg Heym.* The younger poet was always circling around the older one (George). It was an oscillating orbit because Heym simultaneously imitated George to the point of near plagiarism and detested him in a classic instance of a love-hate relationship to one's literary father. While denouncing George at literary cafés as a reactionary "corpse," Heym secretly (as I discovered) tried to get acceptance into the elitist George circle (via Friedrich Wolters). Both poets incarnate the moment of transition from French-influenced "Symbolism" to revolutionary German "Expressionism," although George is usually classified only as a symbolist and Heym only as an Expressionist.

A word on the Heym poems that follow: "With the Ships of Passage" (found among Heym's posthumous notes) was written in two versions, both appearing here in German. The first version is an uninteresting imitation of George's long, unenjambed lines, slow and stately. The second draft has quick, short enjambed lines (though with identical meaning and diction) in an original rhythm later imitated by Gottfried Benn. In this way, a few weeks before drowning, Heym created his own style and perhaps became an even greater poet than George. In a private letter of January 15, 1951, Benn called "With the Ships" the "most beautiful poem of the twentieth century."

The poem "The Wake" was also found among Heym's unpublished papers. Benn called it "one of the three greatest love poems of all time." Its tragic effect derives not merely from what is said literally but from the shattering effect of the broken rhythms, the suddenly truncated lines, the intermittent stark opening trochees, the mood connoted by both imagery and sound. As for Heym's eerie "Demons of the Cities," I discovered in Leningrad that this poem had been translated into Russian by Boris Pasternak in a magazine publication not cited in standard Pasternak bibliographies.

MIT DEN FAHRENDEN SCHIFFEN

(First discarded draft)

Mit den fahrenden Schiffen bin ich geschweift,
Die wir immer durch glänzende Winter gestreift.
Ferne kamen wir weit im insligen Meer.
Trüb war das Jahr. Und der Himmel war leer.

Sage die Stadt wo ich nicht stand im Tor.
Ging dein Fuss hier hindurch, die ich ewig verlor.
Unter dem Abend das flackernde Licht
Hielt ich in vieler fremdes Gesicht.

Bei den Toten ging ich, du warest nicht dort.
Schläfst du doch nicht in dem traurigen Ort.
Und ich zog über Feld. Und die Bäume zu Haupt
Standen herunter, im Dürren entlaubt.

Krähen und Raben habe ich ausgesandt.
Und sie stoben im Himmel über das braune Land.
Sie fielen zur Nacht mir zu Fusse mit traurigem Laut.
Und es hing in den eisernen Schnäbeln nur trockenes Kraut.

Ach deine Stimme so weit. Deine Hand so gebleicht.
Die im Traume mir noch manchmal die Haare streicht.
Alles war schon einmal. Und es kehrt wieder um.
(bricht ab)

Georg Heym

– November 1911

This is Heym's final version, where he keeps the same words much of the time but breaks up the lines (hence the importance of lineation to ear and not only to eye): so as to find his own unique personal style. This style of dreamy trimeters, punctuated now and then with even more wistful dimeters, 38 years later has its haunting rhythms imitated (without acknowledgment) by Gottfried Benn, especially in Benn's poems "Die Dänin" and "Aus Fernen, Aus Reichen" in *Trunkene Flut*, Wiesbaden, Limes Verlag, 1949. The various contrasting versions of the Heym poem (contrasting in rhythm, not in vocabulary or meaning) may be compared in the Heym archive at the University of Hamburg. His unusual final rhythm, his maturest achievement (two months before his death) in delicacy and in control, has few parallels in any language. Aside from the Benn imitations (one could almost say: plagiarisms), this rhythm's effect, though not its precise scansion, is best approximated in the alternating shorter-line stanzas of W.H. Auden's "Shield of Achilles."

MIT DEN FAHRENDEN SCHIFFEN

Mit den fahrenden Schiffen
Sind wir vorübergeschweift,
Die wir ewig herunter
Durch glänzende Winter gestreift.
Ferner kamen wir immer
Und tanzten im insligen Meer;
Weit ging die Flut uns vorbei,
Und Himmel war schallend und leer.

Sage die Stadt,
Wo ich nicht saß im Tor.
Ging dein Fuß da hindurch,
Der die Locke ich schor?
Unter dem sterbenden Abend
Das suchende Licht
Hielt ich; wer kam da hinab?
Ach, ewig ein fremdes Gesicht.

Bei den Toten ich rief,
Im abgeschiedenen Ort,
Wo die Begrabenen wohnen;

Du, ach, warest nicht dort.
Und ich ging über Feld,
Und die wehenden Bäume zu Haupt
Standen im frierenden Himmel
Und waren im Winter entlaubt.

Raben und Krähen
Habe ich ausgesandt,
Und sie stoben im Grauen
Über das ziehende Land.
Aber sie fielen wie Steine
Zur Nacht mit traurigem Laut
Und hielten im eisernen Schnabel
Die Kränze von Stroh und Kraut.

Manchmal ist deine Stimme,
Die im Winde verstreicht,
Deine Hand, die im Traume
Rühret die Schläfe mir leicht;
Alles war schon vorzeiten.
Und kehret wieder sich um.
Gehet in Trauer gehüllet,
Streuet Asche herum.

Georg Heym

– November 1911, published posthumously

WITH THE SHIPS OF PASSAGE

With the ships of passage
Scattered we were and tossed
Downward, always downward
Through winters of glittering frost.
Far we wandered and farther;
In the island sea we played;
Tides left us stranded behind,
And the sky was a droning void.

Name me the town
Where I have failed to wait,
Lighting with my searchlight
Heads passing the gate.
Were these your footsteps, you
Whose locks I'd cut?
None in that dying dusk,
None was the face I sought.

Down to the corpses I called,
Searching the sealed-off lair
Where the buried are huddling;
I called. – O you weren't there.
And I crossed a living field;
And the trees of swaying peak
Stood in the shiver of heaven,
And winter had stripped them bleak.

Crows and ravens
I sent out after you;
Into the gray they scattered,
The land receding below.
But down they fell like millstones,
Fell moaning into night's craw,
And held in their beaks of iron
Garlands of weeds and straw.

Sometimes I feel you calling,
The wind thinning your voice;
Your hands – I feel them in trances
Brushing against my brows;
Long ago all of it happened.
And circles to haunt once more.
Muffled in mournful sackcloth,
Strewing ashes on air.

DIE DÄMONEN DER STÄDTE

Sie wandern durch die Nacht der Städte hin,
Die schwarz sich ducken unter ihrem Fuss.
Wie Schifferbärte stehen um ihr Kinn
Die Wolken schwarz vom Rauch und Kohlenruss.

Ihr langer Schatten schwankt im Häusermeer
Und löscht der Strassen Lichterreihen aus.
Er kriecht wie Nebel auf dem Pflaster schwer
Und tastet langsam vorwärts Haus für Haus.

Den einen Fuss auf einen Platz gestellt,
Den anderen gekniet auf einen Turm,
Ragen sie auf, wo schwarz der Regen fällt,
Panspfeifen blasend in den Wolkensturm.

Um ihre Füsse kreist das Ritornell
Des Städtemeers mit trauriger Musik.
Ein grosses Sterbelied, bald dumpf, bald grell
Wechselt der Ton, der in das Dunkel stieg.

Sie wandern an dem Strom, der schwarz und breit
Wie ein Reptil, den Rücken gelb gefleckt
Von den Laternen, in die Dunkelheit
Sich traurig wälzt die schwarz den Himmel deckt.

Sie lehnen schwer auf einer Brückenwand
Und stecken ihre Hände in den Schwarm
Der Menschen aus, wie Faune, die am Rand
Der Sümpfe bohren in den Schlamm den Arm.

Einer steht auf. Dem weissen Monde hängt
Er eine schwarze Larve vor. Die Nacht,
Die sich wie Blei vom finstern Himmel senkt,
Drückt tief die Häuser in des Dunkels Schacht.

Der Städte Schultern knacken. Und es birst
Ein Dach daraus ein rotes Feuer schwemmt.
Breitbeinig sitzen sie auf seinem First
Und schrein wie Katzen auf zum Firmament.

In einer Stube voll von Finsternissen
Schreit eine Wöchnerin in ihrem Wehn.
Ihr starker Leib ragt riesig aus den Kissen,
Um den herum die grossen Teufel stehn.

Sie hält sich zitternd in der Wehebank.
Das Zimmer schwankt um sie von ihrem Schrei.
Da kommt die Frucht. Ihr Schoss klafft rot und lang
Und blutend reisst er von der Frucht entzwei.

Der Teufel Hälse wachsen wie Giraffen.
Das Kind hat keinen Kopf. Die Mutter hält
Es vor sich hin. In ihrem Rücken klaffen
Des Schrecks Froschfinger, wenn sie rückwärts fällt.

Doch die Dämonen wachsen riesengross.
Ihr Schläfenhorn zerreisst den Himmel rot.
Erdbeben donnert durch der Städte Schoss
Um ihren Huf, den Feuer überloht.

Georg Heym

– in his book *Der Ewige Tag,* 1911

128

The Demons of the Cities

The midnight cities cower underfoot;
The demons trample through the urban graves;
Their skipper-beards, a sprout of smoke and soot,
Bristle like chins of Charons needing shaves.

Creeping on fog-shoes where the pavement drowses
And crawling forward slowly room by room,
Their shadows waver over waves of houses
And gobble street-lights in black gulps of gloom.

Their knees are kneeling on the city towers,
Their feet make footstools of the city squares,
And where the rain strews down its bleakest flowers
Their stormy pipe of Pan rears up and blares.

Around their feet each city's dark refrain
Is circling like a rondo of the waters.
An ode to death. Now faint, now shrill again,
The dirge ebbs into darkness till it falters.

The stream they stroll on is a snaky glow,
Its dim back speckled by the yellow glimmer
The lanterns – blanketed in black-out – throw.
The melancholy reptile wallows dimmer.

Their weight falls heavy on a bridge's railing
Each time their hands fall heavy into swarms
Of urban flesh, as if some faun were flailing
Across a slimy swamp his outstretched arms.

Now one stands up. He hangs a ghoul's black mask
On the white moon. The leaden heavens spill
Down darkly from a heaven darker still,
Crushing the houses in a jet-black cask.

A snapping sound. A city's backbone splits.
A roof cracks open, reddening its rent
With arson. Demons squat on it like cats
And ululate into the firmament.

A spawning mother bawls where midnight billows;
The steep crescendo of each labor pang
Arches her brawny pelvis from its pillows;
Around her the enormous devils throng.

She's tossed yet anchored. Overhead, her bed's
Whole ceiling shakes with howlings of the tortured.
Red furrow – redder, longer. Now the orchard
Brings forth the fruit. It rips her womb to shreds.

The devils' necks are growing like giraffes'.
The baby has no head. The mother lugs
It with her till she faints; a devil laughs;
Her spine is tickled by cold thumbs of frogs.

Tossing their horns, the demons grow so tall
They gash the very sky for blood to plunder.
Through laps of cities roars their earthquake-thunder
While lightning sizzles where their hoofbeats fall.

COMMENT ON HEYM: "THE DEMONS OF THE CITIES"

T he most nightmarish archetype of big-city poetry is Heym's "Die Dämonen der Städte" (The Demons of the Cities), written November 1910, published April 1911 in his book *Der Ewige Tag* (The Eternal Day). Incubi brooding, ever brooding, over urban life: in this vision Heym seems to have rendered the malaise of an asphalt society better than any subsequent writer and to have refuted (in advance) Hart Crane's bridge-invoking hopes to the contrary. Here, as so often, Heym's stately rhymed quatrains are entirely in Stefan George's *style,* imitating (with a few exceptions) George's twofold trend: toward end-stop lines and toward using enjambment (when at all) on the third line of each quatrain. But this time the *subject matter* is not George's at all; these stanzas are not by a Rhinelander of vineyard background but by a street-smart (also street-dreamy) Berliner. This contrast between style and subject makes it a metropolitization of Stefan

George: a spooky synthesis between French Symbolism and German Expressionism.

The poem's original title was *Chimäre*. Its present title derives partly from Baudelaire's demonization of cities (Heym knew George's translation of Baudelaire) and perhaps partly from a 1908 novel, *Dämon Berlin*. Reviewing Heym's book in May 1911, his good friend Ernst Balcke (they drowned together in 1912) wrote that Heym was obsessed by Berlin's "demonic immensity." Heym's diary: "I was afraid of going mad, and a poem (Demons) came to me."

Writing his publisher Rowohlt, Heym put "Demons" at the head of a list of his "best poems." I would instead put his just-before-death trimeter poems, "The Wake" and "With the Ships of Passage," at the head of his best. By that time he had outgrown the slow ponderous George-like pentameters of "Demons." The poem does succeed (he is Germany's Rimbaud, a hillbilly Rimbaud from provincial Silesia) because of its original and apt imagery, its convincing urban mood, and the juggernaut propulsiveness of its rhythms. But they risk monotony, and the luridness at times becomes unintentionally comic, as if Heym here and elsewhere were like that fat boy in Dickens who wants to make your flesh creep.

Readers of "Demons" and of his poems about war are troubled by the ambiguity of Heym's attitude: is he condemning or admiring? As if he were being asked: Which side are you on? The condign word is neither "admiring" nor "condemning" but "fascinated."

This German romantic titanism is shared with his secret mentor, George. Both are ambivalently fascinated by sinister omnipotence (superman, superdemon) and by war. Both identify with Napoleon and have imperial yearnings. It could have been George speaking when Heym confides to his diary in October 1911: "There is only one position that would have suited me: I should have been an emperor." Such ideas in America would be deemed "right wing." In Heym they accompanied his "leftist" revolutionary yearnings to "die on the barricades," red flag in one hand, pistol in the other (as he confides to his diary). Yet Nietzsche warned his adolescent worshippers (of whom Heym was one) that true leadership comes "with the footsteps of doves." The delicate horns of elfland are more powerful than the power-soused jackboot-trample of titanism; all jackboots hide an Achilles' heel. In other words, "With the Ships" is a greater poem than "Demons."

THE WAKE

How dark the veins of your temples;
Heavy, heavy your hands.
Deaf to my voice, already
In sealed-off lands?

Under the light that flickers
You are so mournful and old,
And your lips are talons
Clenched in a cruel mold.

Silence is coming tomorrow
And possibly underway
The last rustle of garlands,
The first air of decay.

Later the nights will follow
Emptier year by year:
Here where your head lay and gently
Ever your breathing was near.

Georg Heym

– In *Books Abroad,* April 1971, I analyze Heym's genius at
length as well as the earlier, here-superseded drafts of this
translation.

132

LETZTE WACHE

(Third version, Sept. 1911)

Wie Dunkel sind deine Schläfen
Und deine Hände so schwer.
Bist du schon weit von dannen
Und hörst mich nicht mehr?

Unter dem flackernden Lichte
Bist du so traurig und alt,
Und deine Lippen sind grausam
In ewiger Starre gekrallt.

Morgen schon ist hier das Schweigen
Und vielleicht in der Luft
Noch das Rascheln von Kränzen
Und ein verwesender Duft.

Aber die Nächte werden
Leerer nun, Jahr um Jahr.
Hier, wo dein Haupt lag, und leise
Immer dein Atem war.

Georg Heym

– from a ms. found posthumously (author drowned in Jan. 1911 at age 24);
latest reprint in *Dichtungen Und Schriften,* Vol. 1, 1964; "one of the three
greatest love poems of all time," according to Gottfried Benn.

The German original of Heym's "White Butterflies," written in 1911, was published posthumously in slightly varied forms in the books *Umbra Vitae*, Leipzig, Rowohlt, 1912 and *Dichtungen*, Munich, Kurt Wolff, 1911 – and in the present form in the definitive *Dichtungen und Schriften*, Gesamtausgabe, Band I Lyrik, Hamburg, Ellermann, 1964.
(Regular or triangular brackets around Heym's handwriting indicate uncertain readings.)

White Butterflies of Night, So Often Near Me

White butterflies of night, so often near me,
Souls of the dead, why are you fluttering so
Over my hand? – on which your wing-beat
Often rubs off a trace of ashes.

You who inhabit urns where drowsing dreams are
Cramped in the narrowness of endless twilight,
Out of your graveyards every sunset
You swarm at me like clamorous bats.

Asleep, I hear a pack of vampires baying;
They sound as if the mournful moon were laughing.
I see deep, deep in empty caverns
Candles the homeless shadows carry.

What is all life but this: a torch's flare-up,
Ringed by the leering densities of dark?
Blackness is reaching out already
To warm thin hands at our thinning fire.

What's life but a small boat in big abysses?
The sea's forlorn, the sky's a glassy stare.
We live the way the moon meanders
Across bare fields and vanishes.

Woe to him who witnessed death in action:
Whenever in the cool autumnal silence
Death sidled up to sweaty sheets of deathbeds
To send the lingerers packing. From their windpipes,

As if from the chilled pipes of a rusty organ,
Their final breath squeaked forth a final gurgle.
He who witnessed death in action
Lugs pale fruits of stony horror.

Who'll open up the realms we're dying toward?
And who the gateway to the monstrous riddle?
What do they see, the dead, what outrage makes them
Roll up their eyes' blind screen of white?

WAS KOMMT IHR, WEIßE FALTER

Was kommt ihr, weiße Falter, so oft zu mir?
Ihr toten Seelen, was flattert ihr also oft
Auf meine Hand, von euerm Flügel
Haftet dann oft ein wenig Asche.

Die ihr bei Urnen wohnt, dort wo die Träume ruhn
In ewigen Schatten gebückt, in dem dämmrigen Raum
Wie in den Grüften Fledermäuse
Die nachts entschwirren mit Gelärme.

Ich höre oft im Schlaf der Vampire Gebell
Aus trüben Mondes Waben wie Gelächter,
Und sehe tief in leeren Höhlen
Der heimatlosen Schatten Lichter.

Was ist das Leben? Eine kurze Fackel
Umgrinst von Fratzen aus dem schwarzen Dunkel
Und manche kommen schon und strecken
Die magren Hände nach der Flamme.

Was ist das Leben? Kleines Schiff in Schluchten
Vergeßner Meere. Starrer Himmel Grauen.
Oder wie nachts auf kahlen Feldern
Verlornes Mondlicht wandert and verschwindet.

Weh dem, der jemals einen sterben sah,
Da unsichtbar in Herbstes kühler Stille
[Der Tod trat an des Kranken feuchtes Bette
Und einen scheiden hieß, da seine Gurgel]

Wie einer rostigen Orgel <Frost und> Pfeifen
Die letzte Luft mit Rasseln stieß von dannen.
Weh dem, der sterben sah. Er trägt für immer
Die weiße Blume bleiernen Entsetzens.

Wer schließt uns auf die Länder nach dem Tode.
Und wer das Tor der ungeheuren Rune.
Was sehn die Sterbenden, daß sie so schrecklich
Verkehren ihrer Augen blinde Weiße.

Georg Heym

[CONCLUSION]

(translation of the untitled poem that concludes Stefan George's last book, *The New Reich*, Berlin, Bondi, 1928)

You flaming arrow pure and slender
You daybreak shy and shimmering
You crowning crest of ancient grandeur
Secret and simple as a spring

Companion on my sunny meadows
Twine of my twilight's eerie wreath
Torch on my path through coming shadows
You cooling breeze you warming breath

You're all my wishing all my thinking
The fragrance I embrace is yours
It's you I'm gulping in my drinking
Inhaling you through all my pores

You crowning crest of ancient grandeur
Aloof and simple as a spring
You flaming arrow pure and slender
You daybreak shy and shimmering.

[DU SCHLANK UND REIN WIE EINE FLAMME]

Du schlank und rein wie eine flamme
Du wie der morgen zart und licht
Du blühend reis vom edlen stamme
Du wie ein quell geheim und schlicht

Begleitest mich aus sonnigen matten
Umschauerst mich im abendrauch
Erleuchtest meinen weg im schatten
Du kühler wind du heisser hauch

Du bist mein wunsch und mein gedanke
Ich atme dich mit jeder luft
Ich schlürfe dich mit jedem tranke
Ich küsse dich mit jedem duft

Du blühend reis vom edlen stamme
Du wie ein quell geheim und schlicht
Du schlank und rein wie eine flamme
Du wie der morgen zart und licht.

Stefan George

[This poem won the Five College Award for the best unpublished translation. Smith, Amherst, U. of Massachusetts, Mt. Holyoke, and Hampshire colleges.]

TRANSLATOR'S COMMENT ON "CONCLUSION"

Stefan George showed his ultimate emphasis on the purely aesthetic by deliberately picking this epiphany of sheer form and sheer melody (written – much earlier – to a German who committed suicide with his lover when ordered to fight for Germany in World War I) as the final poem of his final book, shedding nationalism and his sometimes ominous prophet-robes.

Full circle, back – on one level – to the *l'art pour l'art* of his French *symboliste* origins: after tempest, music.

On another level, what of the lovers' double suicide, not even hinted at in the poem's Parnassian serenity? Is this "omnia vincit amor" – or vincit mors? Certainly not patria – not Mars – vincit omnia.

[AUTUMN'S PARK]

(untitled opening poem of Stefan George's book *The Year of the Soul*, 1897)

Come in the park they say is dead and gaze:
Far shores – green hid their glint until October.
A rift in clouds a blue you dared not hope for
Lights up the fish ponds and the leaf-daubed pathways.

Seek out the tepid gray the warmer yellow
Of boxwood and of birch – the wind is mellow –
Late roses still are clinging to their stem
Garner with care and kiss and garland them.

Don't miss these final asters nor the full
Overfull purple on the unpruned vine.
These last red greens – a light touch binds them twine
Fall's arson with the phoenix wreath of fall.

(German original: first poem of the opening "Nach der Lese" section of George's *Das Jahr Der Seele*, Berlin, Bondi, privately printed 1897, publicly 1899)

Komm in den totgesagten park und schau:
Der schimmer ferner lächelnder gestade,
Der reinen wolken unverhofftes blau
Erhellt die weiher und die bunten pfade.

Dort nimm das tiefe gelb, das weiche grau
Von birken und von buchs, der wind is lau,
Die späten rosen welkten noch nicht ganz,
Erlese küsse sie und flicht den kranz.

Vergiss auch diese letzten astern nicht,
Den purpur um die ranken wilder reben
Und auch was übrig blieb von grünem leben
Verwinde leicht im herbstlichen gesicht.

CONTEXT FOR GEORGE'S POEM "AUTUMN'S PARK"

The book's title, *The Year of the Soul*, was chosen from the last line of the Hoelderlin poem here subsequently translated.

"Thou has thy music too" is Keat's famous invocation of fall. George exalts that season even higher here: a garland that lives, a blue that bursts clouds. In its elegant despair, autumn and not spring is George's characteristic season, as it is also Baudelaire's, whose "phosphorescence of decay" George was at that very time translating.

The German last line of "Autumn's Park" has two ambiguities, "verwinde" and "Gesicht." "Gesicht" means face but here has an older meaning (from "sehen") of "a vision" ("what is seen"). "Verwinde" means to "twine" a wreath. But here it connotes the partly similar "überwinde" (to overcome). The dying of autumn's wreath is being overcome; hence my added word "phoenix."

This fuller meaning of negating autumn's negation comes out in a second poem by George, "Yet," that follows.

[YET]

(translated by Peter Viereck from the German of the autumn section of Stefan George's book *The Year of the Soul*, 1897.)

Scents from the season of losses
Laugh gently from gardens once ours.
Weave, in the hair the wind tosses,
Ivy and last little flowers.

The swaying crops are still gold now,
Perhaps not so tall, not so dense.
The roses still keep you consoled now,
Though glowing more pale, less intense.

Relent about what isn't lent us;
Rejoice at what still stays whole.
Enough what yet it can grant us:
Together one more stroll.

(untitled poem from the autumn section of Stefan George's book *Das Jahr der Seele*, Berlin, Bondi, 1897.)

Es lacht in dem steigenden jahr dir
Der duft aus dem garten noch leis.
Flicht in dem flatternden haar dir
Eppich und ehrenpreis.

Die wehende saat ist wie gold noch,
Vielleicht nicht so hoch mehr und reich,
Rosen begrüssen dich hold noch,
Ward auch ihr glanz etwas bleich.

Verschweigen wir was uns verwehrt ist,
Geloben wir glücklich zu sein,
Wenn auch nicht mehr uns beschert ist
Als noch ein rundgang zu zwein.

[CREDO]

(translated by Peter Viereck from Stefan George's "All die jugend," *Werke*, Volume III, p. 19, untitled poem in his book *The Star of the Covenant*, 1913.)

"Why in drunken play – now flute, now bugle –
Squander like a dance your youthful days?"
To entice your sons of light, O Lord.
For me no human solace; mine the need
To be your singer on my pilgrimage,
Questing till it's you I find in them…
Day and night my quarry's been but this
Since I first awoke to be aware:
You at every twist and turn.

(from Stefan George, *Der Stern des Bundes*, Berlin, Bondi, 1913)

All die jugend floss dir wie ein tanz
Ein berauschtes spiel von horn und flöte?
"Herr so lockt ich deine sonnensöhne.
Menschlich glück verschwor ich um dein lied
Fügte mich der not des wandertumes
Forschte bis ich dich in ihnen fände…
Tag und nacht hab ich nur dies getan
Seit ich eignen lebens mich entsinne:
Dich gesucht auf weg und steg."

TRANSLATOR'S COMMENT ON GEORGE'S "CREDO"

The "Lord" invoked is less Christian than Hellenic. Apollo is implied by "Sonnensöhne," its literal translation being "sun-sons," a tongue-twister that in English would seem an unintended pun, hence better rendered as "sons of light" (with Apollo as god of light). No daughters of light occur in George.

Why has the translator changed the German "flute and bugle" to the English "now flute, now bugle"? To remind modern readers of George's role (clear to his contemporaries but not today) of alternating the public *engagé* voice of bugle with the private *l'art pour l'art* flute.

It was important for the final effect to end this pentameter poem on a trochaic tetrameter.

BLESSED LONGING

(translation of Goethe's "Selige Sehnsucht")

What I tell you, better censor.
Bruit it only to the wiser.
I celebrate what lives intenser:
Life that yearns for death-by-fire.

Nights of loving, nights of cooling,
Where you're begot, where you're begetting,
Seize you with what eerie feeling
When hushed candle-rays are jetting.

Shadows of the dark no longer
Bind you down to be night's plaything.
Now you're launched by newer longing
Up to ever higher mating.

Now no distance is too distant.
Wafted spirit, spellbound flesh.
Moth compelled by flame's insistent
Magnet, you must burn to ash.

And till you confront this test,
This dying-and-becoming,
You'll only be a dismal guest
At the earth's dim gloaming.

SELIGE SEHNSUCHT

Sagt es niemand, nur den Weisen,
Weil die Menge gleich verhöhnet,
Das Lebendge will ich preisen
Das nach Flammentod sich sehnet.

In der Liebesnächte Kühlung,
Die dich zeugte, wo du zeugtest,
Überfällt dich fremde Fühlung
Wenn die stille Kerze leuchtet.

Nicht mehr bleibest du umfangen
In der Finsternis Beschattung,
Und dich reisset neu Verlangen
Auf zu hörerer Begattung.

Keine Ferne macht dich schwierig,
Kommst geflogen und gebannt,
Und zuletzt, des Lichts begierig,
Bist du Schmetterling verbrannt.

Und solang du das nicht hast,
Dieses: Stirb und werde!
Bist du nur ein trüber Gast
Auf der dunklen Erde.

Johann Wolfgang von Goethe, 1814

COMMENT ON GOETHE'S "BLESSED LONGING"

Goethe wrote these stanzas July 31, 1814, during his flight toward inwardness from that time's outward war and politics. The poem was included in his *Westöstlicher Divan*, 1819. Only later did he append the last quatrain, with the unexpected irregularity of its two trimeter lines. The original had appeared earlier and separately under the title "Vollendung" ("Fulfilment"), perhaps a better title, in *Taschenbuch für Damen*. It was inspired by a German translation of the Persian poet Hafiz, whose version likewise has a burned butterfly (actually moth) and the line "The soul burns like the candle."

The German critic von Loeper called Goethe's lyric "the profoundest of all German poems."

WANDERER'S NIGHT SONG
(translation of Goethe's "Wandrers Nachtlied")

To every hill crest
Comes rest.
In every tree crest
The forest
Scarcely draws breath.
Each bird-nest is hushed on the heath.
Wait a bit; soon you
Will find rest too.

Wandrers Nachtlied

Johann Wolfgang von Goethe, 1780-1832

Über allen Gipfeln
Ist Ruh.
In allen Wipfeln
Spürest du
Kaum einen Hauch.
Die Vögelein schweigen im Walde.
Warte nur, balde
Ruhest du auch.

In modern German type and punctuation of today:
WANDRERS NACHTLIED

Über allen Gipfeln

ist Ruh.

Über allen Wipfeln

spürest du

kaum einen Hauch.

Die Vögelein schweigen im Walde.

Warte nur! Balde

ruhest du auch.

COMMENTS ON "WANDERER'S NIGHT SONG"

In 1780 young Goethe penciled these eight lines on the wooden wall of a mountain lodge. Along with Pushkin's "On The Hills Of Georgia," this is the *simplest* great poem in history. So naive-sounding a rhythm, diction, and feeling can only be the product of the most sophisticated craftsmanship. As with the Pushkin poem, translators have either betrayed Goethe's simplicity by cleverness or cloyed it by banality.

To substitute for the resonance of feminine rhyme in German (uninflected English having more masculine rhymes), I've increased the number of rhymes with the key word "rest." And to prevent this increase from becoming monotonous, I've used one rhyme with accent not on "rest" but on the penultimate syllable: "forest" in line four.

To enhance the hush mood by echo, Goethe on line six alliterates the "w" of "schweigen" with the "w" of "Wald." Analogously in line six of the English, "hushed" and "heath" alliterate. This is achieved at the cost of using an eye rhyme (heath, breath) instead of a "perfect" ear rhyme. In denotation, "heath" is not a proper translation of "Wald." The former has mere thickets; the latter is arboreal. But the emotional connotations are partly similar: rustic, unpruned, unmapped, a wilderness for wanderers at night. I don't want to repeat the earlier-used concept of forest and woods. The reader's ear needs the couplet ending in "eath" to escape for just a moment the restless "rest" rhymes.

PARIS, BRIDGE OF THE CARROUSEL

(translated Novermber 26, 2004 by Peter Viereck from Rainer Maria Rilke's "Pont Du Carrousel," *Ausgewaehlte Gedichte* Inset Verlag, Leipzig.)

This blind man on this bridge of carrousel:
Mid-marrow cell, perhaps world's inmost core.
Here nameless vasts take their rotation stations
Around his silence, star-clocks and each star.
He's center of the changing constellations;
All life beside him preens and strays afar.

He is the incorruptible who stayed
Unswayed amid our wayward aberrations.
Landmark, unmovable, austerely grayed,
He is the somber subterranean gate
Beneath a superficial now's impatience.

PONT DU CARROUSEL

Der blinde Mann, der auf der Brücke steht,
grau wie ein Markstein namenloser Reiche,
er ist vielleicht das Ding, das immer gleiche,
um das von fern die Sternenstunde geht,
und der Gestirne stiller Mittelpunkt.
Denn alles um ihn irrt und rinnt und prunkt.

Er ist der unbewegliche Gerechte,
in viele wirre Wege hingestellt;
der dunkle Eingang in die Unterwelt
bei einem oberflächlichen Geschlechte.

Rainer Maria Rilke, 1875-1926

HYACINTH SCENT

(translated by Peter Viereck from the German of Theodor Storm's
"Hyacinthen")

Music far off, but here hushed night commands.
With sleep's aroma, flowers breathe at me.
Of you, of you I think unceasingly.
I long for slumber, but you've got to dance.

It just won't stop. It's raging without pausing,
The candles glaring while the fiddles wail.
The rows of dance keep opening up and closing,
And all are glowing; you alone are pale.

And you must dance, in arms of strangers twirling
Your waist. Don't let them violate your space.
I see the whiteness of your skirt a-whirling
Around your dainty body's whirling grace.

More cloying now, the whiffs of night possess me,
And dreamier now from the exhaling plants.
Now more than ever, thoughts of you obsess me.
I long for slumber; you must stay and dance.

HYAZINTHEN

Fern hallt Musik; doch hier ist stille Nacht,
Mit Schlummerduft anhauchen mich die Pflanzen:
Ich habe immer, immer dein gedacht;
Ich möchte schlafen – aber du mußt tanzen.

Es hört nicht auf, es rast ohn Unterlaß;
Die Kerzen brennen und die Geigen schreien,
Es teilen und es schließen sich die Reihen,
Und alle glühen – aber du bist blaß.

Und du mußt tanzen; fremde Arme schmiegen
Sich an dein Herz; o leide nicht Gewalt!
Ich seh dein weißes Kleid vorüberfliegen
Und deine leichte, zärtliche Gestalt. –

Und süßer strömend quillt der Duft der Nacht
Und träumerischer aus dem Kelch der Pflanzen.
Ich habe immer, immer dein gedacht;
Ich möchte schlafen – aber du mußt tanzen.

Theodor Storm, 1817-88

COMMENT ON STORM'S "HYACINTH SCENT"

The 19th century speaker is waiting out in the dark. Drugged by the erotic flower-scent, he is a bitter window-voyeur of the dance hall, where his beloved must dance. It has been observed that, in the German, the conflicting emotions are expressed by a vowel conflict: the long sensuous "ah" ("schlafen" etc.) versus the shrill jarring "ei" ("die Geigen schreien" etc.). The English language does not have this long "ah" here available, and the literal prosaic translation, "I want to sleep," lacks this crucial sound effect. The nearest I could get to this rich effect is: "I long for slumber."

ONCE MORE

(by Friedrich Nietzsche, 1844-1900; insane since 1889. From his book *Thus Spake Zarathustra*.)

Man, ah lend ear!
What is deep midnight saying? Hear:
"Asleep, asleep
I lay. Now from deep dream I wake.
The world is deep.
And deeper than was deemed by day,
Deep is its ache.
Joy – deeper still than heart's dismay.
Woe says: Forgo!
But all joy wants eternity
– Wants deep, wants deep eternity."

NOCH EINMAL

(from *Also Sprach Zarathustra*)

O Mensch! Gib acht!
Was spricht die tiefe Mitternacht

"Ich schlief, ich schlief – ,
Aus tiefem Traum bin ich erwacht: –
Die Welt is tief,
Und tiefer als der Tag gedacht.

Tief ist ihr Weh –
Lust – tiefer noch als Herzeleid:
Weh spricht: Vergeh!
Doch alle Lust will Ewigkeit
– will tiefe, tiefe Ewigkeit!"

MENON'S LAMENT FOR DIOTIMA

Free rendering from the closing lines of Hoelderlin's long poem, "Menons Klagen um Diotima"

Come, we but dreamt it; already the blood-trailing wings are
Healing; regreened is each single one of the hopes.
Much, much greatness is still ahead; and whoever
Loved as we loved, must heavenward go as we go.
Then guide us, you hours of awe, so youthfully solemn;
You too, you good spirits whose love is to hover with lovers.
Stay with us till we are separate no longer. Unite us
Up there wherever the blest keep watch to return;
There with those sent by the Father, the orbs and the eagles;
There with the muses, the homestead of lovers and heroes;
There
   or down here, on an island dissolving toward spring,
Where we rejoin whom we love in the gardens we loved in,
Where music rings true and April wears daffodils longer
And a year of our soul begins all over again.

Komm! es war wie ein Traum! Die blutenden Fittiche sind ja
 Schon genesen, verjuengt leben die Hoffnungen all.
Grosses zu finden, ist viel, ist viel noch uebrig, und wer so
 Liebte, gehet, er muss, gehet zu Goettern die Bahn.
Und geleitet ihr uns, ihr Weihestunden! ihr ersten,
 Jugendlichen! o bleibt, heilige Ahnungen, ihr
Fromme Bitten! und ihr Begeisterungen und all ihr
 Guten Genien, die gerne bei Liebenden sind;
Bliebt so lange mit uns, bis wir auf gemeinsamem Boden
 Dort, wo die Seligen all niederzukehren bereit,
Dort wo die Adler sind die Gestirne, die Boten des Vaters,
 Dort, wo die Musen, woher Helden und Liebende sind,
Dort uns, oder auch hier, auf tauender Insel begegnen,
 Wo die Unsrigen erst, bluehend in Gaerten gesellt,
Wo die Gesaenge wahr, und laenger die Fruehlinge schoen sind,
 Und von neuem ein Jahr unserer Seele beginnt.

COMMENT ON HOELDERLIN AND THE ART OF TRANSPLANTING

The excerpt here transplanted had impact on Heym, Rilke, and George. All three wrote in awe about him.

In his lifetime Friedrich Hoelderlin (1770-1843, insane from circa 1802) was treated as an odd minor poet. He was condescended to benignly by Goethe and Schiller. The latter mis-spelled his name as "Hoelderlein" ("lein" being a diminutive).

Long almost forgotten, Hoelderlin was rediscovered by Nietzsche, who in 1861 called him his "favorite poet." But the first scholarly research, into his scattered, mostly unpublished poems and papers, did not begin till just before World War I by the George circle, notably Norbert von Hellingrath.

After World War II, there came several new major updatings and revisions by Friedrich Beissner (the vast Stuttgart edition), Adolf Beck, der Rote Stern, etc. Researchers have made both nationalist (Heidegger) and Jacobin claims on him. But his pure poetry itself is what remains the icon of German lyricism today.

Hoelderlin often uses, as here, the caesura'd hexameter. So easy and natural in unaccentual French verse; so hard to control from sprawling in German and English. The most exciting challenge to a Hoelderlin transplanter is rhythm (not rhyme). For example, his famous "Hyperion's Song of Fate" ("Hyperions Schicksalslied," 1798). He best sums up man's fate wordlessly: by the rhythm of water rebounding back and forth in quick two-syllable lines:–

"Hurtled like water
    Between cliff and cliff."
("Wie Wasser von Klippe
    Zu Klippe gerworfen.")

By indenting the second line of each couplet, he shows that life's flow is downhill, not up.

Obvious law: don't deviate; stick to the text (including rhyme sounds and metrics). But for the pedant, lyric's saboteur, text means only denotations, only dictionary meanings. Actually text also means connotations, and these are not literal but vary between languages. In my preceding Storm transplanting, the sensuous somnolent connotation of "ah" in "schlafen" is lost when translated as the denotation "I want to sleep"; instead, "I long for slumber" sounded right.

Because languages have different connotations, a correct equivalent rather than literal translation must sometimes be used. Specific example: I had to translate "in the Greek kalends." In Greek the Latin kalends don't exist; so the word means never or impossible. In English "kalends" means nothing at all to the reader. So my translation was "February 30."

Each rhythm has its own idea, and each idea has its own onomatopoeia. Hence translations must be done from the original poem, by someone steeped in the feel of its language, never from a prose translation done for those unsteeped: a betrayal, and now a frequent one. Good poets speak through their own particular rhythms; Hoelderlin does so above all, in his uniquely compelling ones (sometimes Germanized Pindaric). In his own words, "Rhythm is all."

BIBLIOGRAPHY
Selected writings of Peter Viereck:

Prose Books

Meta-Politics. From the Romantics to Hitler. Alfred A. Knopf, New York, 1941. Out of print.

Meta-Politics: The Roots of the Nazi Mind. G. Putnam Sons, Capricorn, New York, 1965. Out of print.

Conservatism Revisited: The Revolt against Revolt. British hardcover edition. Preface by Sir Duff Cooper, London, 1950. Out of print (available from author).

Conservatism Revisited and the New Conservatism: What Went Wrong? MacMillan Free Press, New York, 1956. Out of print. Reprinted by Greenwood Press, 88 Post Road West, Westport, CT 06881, 1978.

Dream and Responsibility. Test Cases of the Tension between Poetry and Society. University Press of Washington, D.C., 1953, Out of print.

Shame and Glory of the Intellectuals: Babbitt Jr. Versus the Rediscovery of Values. G. Putnam Sons, Capricorn, New York, 1965. Out of print. Reprinted by Greenwood Press, Westport, CT, 1978, with supplement on "The Radical Right: From McCarthy to Goldwater."

Conservatism from John Adams to Churchill. A History and Anthology. Van Nostrand, 1956. Out of print. Reprinted by Greenwood Press, Westport, CT, 1978.

The Unadjusted Man: Reflections on the Distinction between Conserving and Conforming. Beacon Press, 1956. Out of print. Reprinted by Greenwood Press, Westport, CT, 1973.

"Conservatism." A long historical monograph in the 15th edition, 1979-1986, of *The Encyclopedia Britannica.*

Metapolitics: From Wagner and the German Romantics to Hitler. Transaction Publishers, Somerset, NJ, 2003.

Unadjusted Man in the Age of Overadjustment. Transaction Publishers, Somerset, NJ, 2004.

Conservatism Revisited: The Revolt against Ideology. Transaction Publishers, Somerset, NJ, January 2005.

Strict Wildness: Discoveries in History and Poetry. Transaction Publishers, Somerset, NJ, July, 2005.

From John Adams Through Churchill: Annotated Anthology of Conservative Thinkers. Transaction Publishers, Somerset, NJ, 2005.

Poetry Books

Terror and Decorum. Scribner's, 1948. Awarded Pulitzer Prize for Poetry. Out of print. Reprinted by Greenwood Press, Westport, CT, 1972

Strike through the Mask: New Lyrical Poems. Scribner's, 1950. Out of print. Reprinted by Greenwood Press, Westport, CT, 1972

The First Morning. Scribner's, 1952. Out of print. Reprinted by Greenwood Press, Westport, CT, 1972.

The Persimmon Tree: New Lyrics and Pastorals. Scribner's, 1956. Out of print. Reprinted by University Microfilms, Ann Arbor, MI.

New and Selected Poems, 1932-1967. Selections from five books with frontispiece by the Spanish painter Fernando Zobel, 1967 first edition, Bobbs-Merrill, New York. Out of print. 1980 reprint available from University Microfilms, 300 North Zeeb Road, Ann Arbor, MI 48106 or 30 Mortimer Street, London, England WIN 7RA.

Archer in the Marrow. The Applewood Cycles of 1967-1987. W.W. Norton Company, New York, 1987. Out of print.

Tide and Continuities: Last and First Poem, 1995-1938, with a preface in verse by Joseph Brodsky. University of Arkansas Press, Fayetteville, AK, 1995.

Transplantings. Stefan George and Georg Heym, Englished and Analyzed. With Reflections on Modern Germany, on Poetry, and on the Craft of Translation. Work in progress.

Door. Higganum Hill Books, Higganum, CT, June, 2005.

Verse Drama

The Tree Witch. Staged 1961 by the Poets Theater at Harvard University's Loeb Theater. Scribner's, 1961. Out of print. Reprinted by Greenwood Press, Westport, CT, 1973.

OpComp. A modern medieval miracle play. Work in progress.

About Peter Viereck

Henault, Marie. *Peter Viereck, Historian and Poet.* Twayne Press, New York, 1969. Out of print. College and University Press, New Haven, CT, 1971. Out of print.

About the Author

Peter Viereck was born in New York City in 1916. He attended Horace Mann High School and graduated Summa cum Laude from Harvard in 1937. He won 2 battle stars in The U.S. Army overseas in World War II.

Viereck was awarded the Pulitzer Prize for poetry in 1949. He taught history and poetry at Mt Holyoke College and was visiting professor at Oxford, England and the University of Florence, Italy.

In this volume, the opening poem, *Autobiog*, presents his *weltanschauung*, and comments on his life and times. The *Bibliography* lists his extensive work in history, philosophy and poetry as well as his many awards.

Writing in *Agni* magazine, the Nobel Laureate Joseph Brodsky called Viereck's poetry, "the best in America today."